ENJOY THE SILENCE

A 30 DAY EXPERIMENT IN LISTENING TO GOD

MAGGIE ROBBINS
DUFFY ROBBINS

ZONDERVAN™

GRAND RAPIDS, MICHIGAN 49530 USA

www.invertbooks.com

Enjoy the Silence: A 30-Day Experiment in Listening to God
Copyright © 2005 by Maggie Robbins & Duffy Robbins

Youth Specialties Products, 300 South Pierce Street, El Cajon, CA 92020 are
published by Zondervan, 5300 Patterson Avenue Southeast, Grand Rapids, MI 49530.

Library of Congress Cataloging-in-Publication Data
Robbins, Maggie, 1953-
 Enjoy the silence : a 30-day experiment in listening to God / by
Maggie Robbins and Duffy Robbins.
    p. cm.
 Includes index.
 ISBN 0-310-25991-6 (pbk.)
 1. Bible--Reading 2. Christian youth--Religious life. I. Robbins,
Duffy. II. Title.
 BS617.R55 2005
 242'.63--dc22

2005010112

Unless otherwise indicated, all Scripture quotations are taken from the Holy Bible:
New International Version (North American Edition), copyright © 1973, 1978, 1984
by International Bible Society. Used by permission of Zondervan Publishing House.

"Word" by Madeleine L'Engle. *From Lines Scribbled on An Envelope While
Riding the 104 Bus* by Madeleine L'Engle. Copyright © 1969 by Crosswicks, Ltd.
Reprinted by permission of Lescher & Lescher, Ltd.

Web site addresses listed in this book were current at the time of publication. Please
contact Youth Specialties via e-mail (YS@YouthSpecialties.com) to
report URLs that are no longer operational and replacement URLs if available.

Editorial direction by Doug Davidson
Edited by Randy Southern
Proofread by Ivy Beckwith and Anna Hammend
Cover design by Burnkit
Interior design by Mark Novelli, IMAGO MEDIA
Printed in the United States

14 15 16 • 25 24 23 22 21 20 19 18 17

TABLE OF CONTENTS

WORD

I, who live by words, am
            wordless when
I try my words in prayer. All
            language turns
To silence. Prayer will take my words
            and then
Reveal their emptiness. The stifled voice
            learns
To hold its peace, to listen with the
            heart
To silence that is joy, is adoration.
The self is shattered, all words torn
            apart
In this strange patterned time of
            contemplation
That, in time, breaks time, breaks
            words, breaks me,
And then, in silence leaves me
            healed and mended.
I leave returned to language, for I see
Through words, even when all
            words are ended,
I, who live by words, am
            wordless when
I turn me to the Word to pray.
            Amen.

—Madeleine L'Engle
Lines Scribbled on An Envelope While Riding the 104 Bus

CHAPTER ONE

WHOLLY LISTENING

We'd been to this church several times, so the offer didn't catch either of us totally off guard. On the other occasions I had spoken at Mount Oak Church in suburban Washington, D.C., Maggie and I had opportunities to meet some of the folks in the congregation. We knew many of them held important and interesting government jobs. It was not unusual on a Sunday morning to be ushered to your seat by a Pentagon consultant, listen to a testimony by an FBI agent, or hear an offertory solo by a congressional aide.

But Steve Evans had a particularly intriguing job. He was in charge of all Secret Service agents working in the White House.

He approached us after the Sunday evening service and offered an invitation. He said he would like the two of us to come to the White House the next morning to meet the president of the United States.

Of course we were blown away. We couldn't believe it. We just kept thinking, "Gosh, what a treat this will be for the president!" So we said, "Great, let's do it!"

Standing in the back of the church, we worked through the logistics of the next morning. Steve made it very clear we needed to meet him at the west gate of the White House promptly at 7:30 a.m.—and we had to be out by 8:15 a.m. It seems there was a cabinet meeting scheduled for 8:15, and Steve had a sneaky suspicion the cabinet members wouldn't appreciate our presence in the room during the meeting.

He told us we'd have to leave the home where we were staying by 6:30 a.m. if we were going to make it to the White House by 7:30. That meant rise-and-shine no later than 5:30!

That Sunday night we went to bed at our friends' house with our heads spinning. We couldn't believe we were going to be standing in the Oval Office in eight short hours. It took us awhile to settle down to sleep, but finally we drifted off.

In what seemed like the middle of the night, we were awakened by a ringing phone. We couldn't figure out who would be calling at such an hour, but since it wasn't our phone, we ignored it. We heard footsteps crossing the kitchen floor to answer the phone. A moment later Carol, our hostess, knocked on our bedroom door and said, "Duffy, are you awake? Telephone for you. It's the White House!"

I opened the door, still half asleep, took the phone from her, and said, "Mr. President, I hope you're not going to ask us to stick around for the cabinet meeting tomorrow morning. We've got things to do."

I was greeted by an urgent voice. "Duffy, is that you? Where are you? Do you know what time it is?"

My brain was still lingering in the Twilight Zone, so I asked, "Who is this?"

"It's Steve Evans," was the reply. "Duffy, it's 7:45. I was calling just to make sure you guys were on your way. If you haven't left yet, there's no way you're going to get down here in time. We're going to have to cancel the whole thing this morning. I'm sorry. Maybe the next time you come to Mount Oak, we can set something up."

By the time I hung up the phone, my wife knew something was up. She heard only my end of the conversation, but she could tell something wasn't right. When I got back to bed, she asked what the problem was.

"Maggie," I said, "I don't know how to say this, but you're married to one of the only guys in the country who slept through a chance to meet the president of the United States."

I couldn't see the expression on Maggie's face, but I knew exactly what she was thinking. She was thinking—well, she was thinking exactly the same thing you're thinking as you read this story: *What a complete idiot!*

But before you close this book in disgust, let me make two comments about this episode.

Number one: It never happened. We made it up.

Number two: Actually, it did happen. In fact, it happened this morning. And it happens every day to millions of people. It's probably happened to you.

Not that you would sleep through a chance to go to the Oval Office and meet the president of the United States. Nobody's that stupid.

But people just like you—just like us—on days just like this one, pass up the opportunity to enter the throne room of almighty God and talk to the Creator of the universe. Every new day offers each of us a chance to get out of bed and spend some quality time with our heavenly Father. But most of us blow it off for a few extra minutes of sleep.

That's a pretty sobering thought. But it shouldn't make you feel like a disgusting, spiritually impaired, sleep monger. That's not the purpose of this book. After all, meeting with God every morning isn't some religious hoop you have to jump through in order to earn his love. We spend time with God because he loves us *already*—unconditionally—and because we want to develop and deepen our relationship with him. Heck, it doesn't even have to happen in the morning! (Can we get an "Amen"?)

AN AUDIENCE WITH THE KING

The purpose of this book is to invite you into the presence of God, to help you find a practical way to listen and speak to the One who desperately wants a deeper relationship with you. The practical method we're talking about is a devotional exercise called *lectio divina*, two Latin words that literally mean "divine reading." At the heart of this exercise is a very simple notion: *God wants to speak to us, but in order to hear him, we have to be willing to listen.* (For more about God's desire to make himself known to us, check out Psalm 19:1-4; John 1:1,14; Romans 1:18-21; 2:14-15.)

Just listen. Sounds simple, right? Wrong. You see, we live in a loud world, and often God speaks quietly.

> The Lord said, "Go out and stand on the mountain in the presence of the Lord, for the Lord is about to pass by." Then a great and powerful wind tore the mountains apart and shattered the rocks before the Lord, but the Lord was not in the wind. After the wind there was an earthquake, but the Lord was not in the earthquake. After the earthquake came a fire, but the Lord was not in the fire. And *after the fire came a gentle whisper.* (1 Kings 19:11-12)

There, *in that whisper*, was the voice of God.

FINDING QUIET SPACE IN A LOUD WORLD

Suppose you're on a retreat and your youth leader gives you a passage of Scripture to read with these instructions: "Go find a place where you can't see anybody else and read this passage at least three times. Give yourself at least half an hour. Stay in that place and, in the silence and solitude, see what happens."

Let's say you find a place in the woods next to a babbling brook. The birds are singing. The breeze is gently blowing. You find the perfect tree stump, take a seat, open your Bible, and read the passage. Then you read it again. And, for good measure, you read it a third time. After trying really hard to be quiet for as long as you can, you check your watch.

Only five minutes have passed.

Oh, man, what the heck are you going to do for another 25 minutes?

You think through your options: study the maps in the back of your Bible, draw mustaches on the pictures of the little children on Jesus' lap, check to see if there are any illustrations in Song of Songs, or look for secret codes in the Book of Revelation. Finally, you decide to read your assigned passage once again.

This time, you find there's one particular word or phrase that keeps jumping out at you. You didn't think much about it on the first pass. But on your fourth reading, it begins to stick in your heart. You start to think about it.

There are still distractions over the next 25 minutes—the sounds of the forest, the ants crawling across a nearby log, the shadow of what appears to be Bigfoot crashing through the woods—but you keep bringing your attention back to that word, that phrase. And in that place of intentional listening, in that carved-out space of quiet, you sense God is speaking to you. That is *lectio divina*.

It's not a complicated spiritual discipline. All you have to do is read a passage of Scripture slowly and repeatedly, and then give God the space and time to speak to your heart through that passage.

Lectio divina isn't just an impressive name for an everyday Bible study or quiet time. With *lectio* the emphasis is not on content but on contemplation. *Lectio* is a discipline inviting us to listen at a deeper level. Bible study is an activity—it's something you *do*. You read a chapter, you underline key verses and words, you make notes in the margins.

Lectio begins with a word, a verse, a picture, a hint of God. Its goal is to move us from listening with the head to listening with the heart, from activity to receptivity. The emphasis is not on speaking or praying to God. Or thinking great thoughts about God. Or logging time on a spiritual stopwatch. Or notching a few more Bible facts on the walls of our brains. *Lectio divina* is a devotional exercise where the key is listening.

Lectio divina is about creating the space and time for God to speak to us. One writer described it as an exercise in which the mind meets the heart, so the heart can meet God. It's a quiet time that places a strong emphasis on creating *time* for *quiet*.

ANTHONY OF THE DESERT

The practice of *lectio divina* dates back almost 18 centuries to a young Egyptian man named Anthony (251-356). Anthony was, what you might call, a hard-core believer. One day he heard a sermon on Jesus' words in Mark 10:21: "Go, sell everything you have.... Then come, follow me." And that's what Anthony did. He stuck around long enough for his kid sister to finish school, then he sold everything he owned and took off for the desert. And that's where he lived in solitude for the rest of his life. His only nourishment was bread and water—which he never tasted before sunset and sometimes tasted only once every three or four days. The only clothing he wore was sackcloth and sheepskin. The only thing he did from sunset to sunrise was pray.

Believe it or not, when other people heard about Anthony of the Desert and his lifestyle of silence and solitude, they thought it sounded like a good idea. An entire monastic community sprang up in the desert under the instruction and encouragement of Anthony and other "desert fathers and mothers." The people in the community were seeking to separate themselves from every distraction and obstacle that might interfere with their ability to hear God. They weren't just looking for cheap property and a high-carb diet. They were wrestling with the same issues followers of Jesus wrestle with today—stuff like wealth, lust, greed, success, and popularity. More than anything else, they wanted to hear God.

Now you might be thinking, "Wait a minute, Anthony of the Desert sounds like a nickname from WWE SmackDown!, and my folks will kill me if I run away to the desert, and my school has a strict dress code that doesn't permit sheepskin." But never mind any of that.

Eighteen centuries after Anthony, we can still practice habits that help us step away from the noise, stress, and distractions of the world in order to create silence and space for God to speak to our hearts. But those habits require discipline—namely, the spiritual discipline of *lectio divina*.

LECTIO DIVINA: THE PRACTICE OF WHOLLY LISTENING

When Maggie and I were in middle school, seventh graders were required to take dance lessons as part of gym class. And let me tell you, those dance lessons were among the most awkward moments of our teenage years. You can imagine the passion in the air when the gym teachers called on five seventh-grade guys to ask some poor girls to dance. Some of the guys were still convinced that girls had cooties, so they weren't exactly chivalrous. In fact, most of the guys walked back and forth in front of the equally uncomfortable girls looking for a partner with all the tact of a sheik shopping for a camel.

The worst part, though, was learning the dance steps. One-two-three-slide, one-two-three-get off your partner's foot. You've been there. The gym teachers told us how wonderful it was for us to learn such necessary social graces, and how exotic it would be to glide across the floor with our partners. But most of us were so busy watching our feet, we barely even noticed we had partners. To us, the ritual of romance and grace was reduced to three steps and a slide.

You may feel the same sense of awkwardness in trying to master the steps of a spiritual exercise. We all know what it's like to hear mature Christians talk about their wonderful times of prayer and meditation; meanwhile, we're floundering with "one—pray, two—read, three—be totally confused by what we just read, four—eat bread and drink water, five—slide, six—doze off, seven—go back to one." But *spiritual disciplines are not about getting all the steps right. They are about developing habits that will help us gaze into the face of our partner, Jesus, the Lord of the Dance.*

Obviously there's a lot more to *lectio divina* than a series of steps. No one is suggesting just going through the motions described in this book will usher you in to the throne room of God. Working really hard to listen is like trying really hard to fall asleep. Sometimes just the act of concentration itself becomes a distraction. We must remember it's not a matter of simply deciding to listen. God must decide to speak, also.

But we can prepare ourselves to listen well. Just as we might get ready for a special meal with friends—setting aside a time, inviting guests, setting the table, taking care to set the right atmosphere, eliminating any distractions—there is much we can do to prepare for our Divine Guest, to let God know he is welcome and his visit is expected eagerly.

A French Benedictine monk named Dom Marmion describes *lectio divina* in terms of four steps: "We read *(lectio)* under the eye of God *(meditatio)* until the heart is touched *(oratio)* and leaps to flame *(contemplatio)*." Understandably, when we first read those words—*lectio, meditatio, oratio, and contemplatio*—they seem strange to us. Like something off the dessert menu at Bertucci's. However, those four steps help us develop a habit of excavating our hearts and clearing our minds so God can take us to new depths in our relationship with him.

Step One: *Lectio*

Saint Benedict described *lectio divina* as cultivating the ability to listen deeply, to hear "with the ear of our heart." In other words we open the door to our heavenly Guest by listening.

Lectio means reading. Not reading to get through something. Not reading to get the facts. But reading to get focused. Reading slowly. Refusing to be hurried. This type of reading is a form of gentle listening. Just as you can't fully appreciate all the facets of a diamond by driving by it in a car, you can't fully appreciate a Bible text by cruising past it at full speed on your way to the next paragraph.

To help you slow down, we've installed some verbal "speed bumps" throughout the readings in this book. You will come across phrases like "Read slowly," "Don't hurry through these verses," and "Take your time with these words." One of the real keys to *lectio* is expectant reading. God *is* going to meet you in this text, but it likely will not be through a pop-up message or an IM flashing across the bottom of the page. Sometimes he will speak loudly and clearly, but often you will need to listen for his "still, small whisper."

Step Two: *Meditatio*

Meditatio, or meditation, is a concept that seems a little weird to some people. That's because the word is used so many different ways and in so many different contexts. Does it involve chanting? Closing our eyes and trying to communicate with a rainbow? Going into a closet and smoking oatmeal?

Biblically speaking, meditation is taking time to think about something, to savor it, to deeply consider its meaning. For example, as the amazing events of the first Christmas unfolded around the Virgin Mary, we are told she *"treasured up all these things and pondered them in her heart"* (Luke 2:19). Meditation is the act of pondering something in your heart.

Contemplative writers have compared meditation to the process of a cow chewing its cud. If you're unfamiliar with the bovine digestive system, we'll tell you cows have four stomachs. After food has been digested in stomach number one, the cow must, er, bring it back up into its mouth so it can be broken into smaller pieces for its adventure in stomach number two. It is that process of chewing and re-chewing that makes it look like a grateful farmer has rewarded every cow in his herd with a pack of gum to enjoy while waiting for the next milking.

Meditatio is taking time to chew and re-chew a passage of Scripture. Don't just read it once and buzz on to the next mouthful. Take in the text, consume it, and then...chew on it some more. Joshua 1:8 reminds us of the importance of this process: "Do not let this Book of the Law depart from your mouth; meditate on it day and night, so that you may be careful to do everything written in it. Then you will be prosperous and successful."

Have you ever eaten a peanut-butter-and-jelly sandwich that has too much peanut butter on it? You bite into the thing and it's like oral quicksand. You don't just swallow and move on to the corn chips. You chew, and then you chew some more. You take your time with each bite. That's *meditatio.*

Step Three: *Oratio*

After having listened carefully and read the text slowly, the next step in this dance of communion with God is *oratio*— talking to God in prayer. If hearing the Bible and meditating on its texts allows God to talk to us, *oratio*, or prayer, allows us to talk back to God. *Oratio* is conversation that informs us and shapes us.

Contemplative writers call this shaping process *consecration*. And, though that sounds like a physical conditionresulting from a lack of roughage in the diet, it actually idescribes the process of offering ourselves to God in obedience. It's the response of an open heart that hears the voice of God.

As you move through the readings in this book, you'll notice we've given you questions and thoughts that might prompt you in your conversations with God. We've also provided some space in the book for you to journal your responses. You can write your thoughts directly in the book, or you may wish to use your own journal or notebook. It doesn't matter.

What does matter is that we respond to God in conversation and prayerful dialogue. It may be a response of praise, a response of thanksgiving, a response of petition (asking for God's help), a response of confession ("God, I'm sorry—I blew it") or a response of commitment ("God, I have wholly listened; now help me be more holy, and more wholly yours in this area of my life").

First, we open ourselves to God with concentrated listening. Then we respond to God with consecrated obedience. It is this rhythm of conversation and consecration that drives *oratio*, the third stage of *lectio divina*.

Step Four: *Contemplatio*

The final stage of *lectio divina* is *contemplatio*, or contemplation. Resting in the presence of God. Imagine a small child nestled in her father's lap, saying nothing, but completely content in the closeness of that moment. Hearing his slow breathing. Feeling the stubble of his beard. Comforted by the steady arms and strong hands cradling her head.

Or imagine two friends sitting next to a campfire. They've talked about the day's hike—adventures shared, vistas seen, wrong trails taken. They've talked about where the journey led them and where it may lead them tomorrow. Now they share the silence, staring into the flames together, quietly, contentedly. Like basking in the rays of warm sunshine, *contemplatio* is basking in the presence of the Father. It is a time of silence, allowing our intimacy with God to go beyond the place words can take us.

In some ways this may be the most difficult part of the *lectio* exercise because it feels like we ought to be *doing* something. Father Luke Dysinger, a Benedictine monk, describes it in these terms:

> In contemplation we cease from interior spiritual doing and learn simply to be, that is to rest in the presence of our loving Father. Just as we constantly move back and forth in our exterior lives between speaking and listening, between questioning and reflecting, so in our spiritual lives we must learn to enjoy the refreshment of simply being in God's presence.

Throughout the readings you'll notice instructions to "linger," "bask," and "savor." These are words inviting us to experience and enjoy the embrace of the Father.

DANCE, CHILDREN, DANCE

Of course, if all your attention is focused on getting the right steps down, you're missing the whole point. The goal of this book is not to get you to dance the dance called *lectio divina*. The goal is to help you to grow closer to the God who invites you to join him in the dance—whether it's a salsa, a waltz, a tango, a *pas de deux*, or the cha-cha slide. Someday you may not even have to watch your feet. Your time with God will be as spontaneous and natural as your time with any other close friend. Until that time our prayer is that the readings in these pages will get you on the dance floor.

CHAPTER TWO

HOW TO USE THIS BOOK

Probably the number one reason most of us aren't enjoying regular, quality time with God is we don't know how to do it. We sit in front of our Bibles trying to find something we understand and come across a passage like "...and for the parbar on the west there were four at the road and two at the parbar..." (1 Chronicles 26:18, RSV). And we ask, "What in the world does that mean—and what in the world am I doing here?"

If we actually thought we were going to be ushered into the Oval Office to meet the president, most of us would find a way to crawl out of bed and get there. The reason we don't line up at the west gate of the White House every morning is that we know we probably won't be admitted. Likewise, the reason most of us don't set aside a few minutes every day to enter the throne room of almighty God is we're not very confident we'll get to meet him.

Enjoying silence in the presence of God takes practice. Don't be discouraged if your early attempts at *lectio divina* are more about silence than they are about the presence of God. Remember, God *wants* to speak to you.

Here are some practical tips that might help you turn your good intentions into a consistent habit of wholly listening.

You need a time. If you're really serious about doing *lectio divina*, you need to set aside a time to do it. It's like spending time with any other friend. The first detail you need to iron out is when you will get together.

There is no "right" time of day to meet with God. If you're not a morning person, you don't have to do it in the morning. You could schedule it at night, right before you go to sleep. (Just make sure you don't do it *while* you're going to sleep.) You could meet God in study hall at school. Or during lunch. Just make sure you allow yourself time to be unhurried. God doesn't talk fast.

We suggest you begin by allowing about 20 minutes for *lectio divina*. As you desire more time, you can always increase it. Some people get so fired up about the idea of doing spiritual disciplines that they start with a totally unrealistic commitment ("I'm going to get up tomorrow morning at 1:00 a.m. and memorize the entire Old Testament before school"). Then they end up bailing out of the commitment by the second day. Next thing you know, these modern-day "desert fathers" and "desert mothers" just become deserters. Don't let that happen to you.

You need a place. One way to build some consistency in your contemplative life is to have a specific place to meet God each day. You can do it in your room, at your desk, in front of a fireplace, or behind your house. The actual setting is no big deal. No one is suggesting that you build a little shrine in your bedroom with flowers, candles, a Third Day album, and this book. But it should be a place that is quiet and relatively private.

This may sound kind of hokey, but your posture also makes a difference. You'll want to be comfortable as you prepare for your devotional time: seated in a decent chair, feet flat on the floor, surrounded by good lighting. Just make sure you're not so comfortable that you nod off into "involuntary prayer."

You need a plan. The daily readings in this book follow a format based on the four stages of *lectio divina.* Within each reading you'll find the following:

LISTENING

Each entry begins with a passage from Scripture. As you work through the entries, you'll be asked to read and re-read passages. Typically, in a *lectio* exercise, you'll read a passage slowly at least three times. Don't try any shortcuts here. Chew and re-chew!

You'll find one or two selected verses in each passage printed in italics. The italics indicate the portion of the passage that will be the primary focus of the meditation. *Lectio divina,* in the truest sense, wouldn't normally involve a text selected in advance. You would read through an entire passage two or three times and, then, wait for a word or a phrase to stick in your mind. As you become more comfortable with this spiritual discipline, you may want to pick your own focus verses. However, for the readings in this book, we'll give you a particular portion of the passage on which to focus.

MEDITATION

The second portion of each entry will help you in your meditation on the passage. This is the heart of the exercise. In some instances you'll be instructed to pause during meditation as you take time to re-read the passage, journal your thoughts, or simply be quiet. These verbal speed bumps will help you slow your pace and maintain your rhythm of concentration, meditation, and consecration.

FURTHER ON, DEEPER IN

As you read the meditation, you'll notice places where you're instructed to write your thoughts, your concerns, and your reflections. Think of this third stage as the "talking back" portion of your dialogue with God. We've provided space within each entry for you to do that. You may choose to make your entries in your own devotional journal or notebook. That's okay, too.

COMPANIONS ON THE JOURNEY

We've ended each entry with a quotation to give you something to think about as you close your meditation. These quotations come from a wide variety of authors with many different backgrounds, nationalities, eras, and church traditions. Yet the writers share one thing in common; each one was listening for God. Think of these folks as fellow travelers with you on the journey into the heart of God. Wherever possible, we've included some information about each writer and the original source of the quotation.

You may find some of these words for contemplation are as helpful as the meditation itself. Think of them as the "cool down" portion of the exercise.

WALK SOFTLY AND CARRY A BIG HEART

You may be using this book on your own or as part of a small group. In any case your willingness to venture into these new places of intimacy with God says something good about your spiritual journey. Walk confidently, be steady in your pace, and notice the sights along the way as you discover new ground in your relationship with God. Savor the space this book offers you to expand and explore a deeper relationship with Jesus. It's going to be an awesome experience. Enjoy the silence!

DAY 1

LISTENING

Luke 8:4-15

4 While a large crowd was gathering and people were coming to Jesus from town after town, he told this parable:

5 "A farmer went out to sow his seed. As he was scattering the seed, some fell along the path; it was trampled on, and the birds of the air ate it up.

6 Some fell on rock, and when it came up, the plants withered because they had no moisture.

7 Other seed fell among thorns, which grew up with it and choked the plants.

8 Still other seed fell on good soil. It came up and yielded a crop, a hundred times more than was sown."
When he said this, he called out, "He who has ears to hear, let him hear."

9 His disciples asked him what this parable meant.

10 He said, "The knowledge of the secrets of the kingdom of God has been given to you, but to others I speak in parables, so that, 'though seeing, they may not see; though hearing, they may not understand.'

11 "This is the meaning of the parable: The seed is the word of God.

12 Those along the path are the ones who hear, and then the devil comes and takes away the word from their hearts, so that they may not believe and be saved.

13 Those on the rock are the ones who receive the word with joy when they hear it, but they have no root. They believe for a while, but in the time of testing they fall away.

14 The seed that fell among thorns stands for those who hear, but as they go on their way they are choked by life's worries, riches and pleasures, and they do not mature.

15 But the seed on good soil stands for those with a noble and good heart, who hear the word, retain it, and by persevering produce a crop."

MEDITATION

This is a meditation on your hearing skills—your ability to listen. Read the passage once slowly and *simply listen* as Jesus tells the story of the three soils.

[Pause to read.]

Now read it a second time. This time *listen with your imagination.* Imagine the scene Jesus is describing. Imagine the seed. Imagine what each of the soils might have looked like. Imagine what became of each of the soils ("plants withered," "choked," etc.).

[Pause to read.]

Now read it a third time and *listen with your heart.* Surely this is what Jesus meant when he said, "He who has ears to hear, let him hear" (verse 8). Listen with an openness to receive, to grow, and to respond. This time read slowly. Pause for at least a minute of silence after each of the three soils is described and listen with your heart.

[Pause to read.]

Notice the word *heart* is mostly made up of the word *hear.* Maybe it's just a quirk of linguistic coincidence. But maybe it's a hint of something critically important. In the story Jesus told, the seed scattered in each place is the same: the Word of God (verse 11). The soil, although different in each place, symbolizes the heart. (Notice in verse 12 the phrase, "from their hearts," and in verse 15, the phrase, "a noble and good heart.")

Through this story Jesus invites us to examine the soil of our hearts. Is it hard soil—unwilling to hear? Is it choked soil—distracted by the noise and demands of everyday life? Is it good soil—ready to receive, ready to retain, ready to reproduce? You may want to journal your thoughts before you go on.

[Pause to journal.]

Finish your meditation exercise with this *lectio* experience: Close your eyes and imagine your own heart as a field of soil. What sort of soil is it? Is it rocky soil, hard of hearing? Is it soil being choked by thorns and stress? Is it soft soil, the kind that's ready to listen and respond?

Imagine the Gardner's hands right now working with your heart. Is he breaking the ground? Clearing the overgrowth? Seeding? Weeding? Watering? Cultivating? Allow yourself some space and time to listen. Then write your reflections in the following journal area.

Those who have ears, let them hear.

FURTHER ON, DEEPER IN

Use the space below and on the following page to share your own thoughts and reflections.

COMPANIONS ON THE JOURNEY

CULTIVATE MY HEART, LORD, SO I MAY CATCH EVERY
WORD THAT FALLS FROM HEAVEN—EVERY SYLLABLE OF ENCOURAGEMENT,
EVERY SENTENCE OF REBUKE, EVERY PARAGRAPH OF INSTRUCTION,
EVERY PAGE OF WARNING. HELP ME TO CATCH THESE WORDS AS THE SOFT,
FERTILE SOIL CATCHES SEEDS.

—KEN GIRE, U.S. AUTHOR AND SPEAKER

DAY 2

LISTENING

Jeremiah 31:16-25

16 This is what the Lord says: "Restrain your voice from weeping and your eyes from tears, for your work will be rewarded," declares the Lord. "They will return from the land of the enemy.

17 So there is hope for your future," declares the Lord. "Your children will return to their own land.

18 "I have surely heard Ephraim's moaning: 'You disciplined me like an unruly calf, and I have been disciplined. Restore me, and I will return, because you are the Lord my God.

19 After I strayed, I repented; after I came to understand, I beat my breast. I was ashamed and humiliated because I bore the disgrace of my youth.'

20 Is not Ephraim my dear son, the child in whom I delight? Though I often speak against him, I still remember him. Therefore my heart yearns for him; I have great compassion for him," declares the Lord.

21 *Set up road signs; put up guideposts.* Take note of the highway, the road that you take. Return, O Virgin Israel, return to your towns.

22 How long will you wander, O unfaithful daughter? The Lord will create a new thing on earth— a woman will surround a man."

23 This is what the Lord Almighty, the God of Israel, says: "When I bring them back from captivity, the people in the land of Judah and in its towns will once again use these words: 'The Lord bless you, O righteous dwelling, O sacred mountain.'

24 People will live together in Judah and all its towns— farmers and those who move about with their flocks.

25 I will refresh the weary and satisfy the faint."

MEDITATION

Picture the road on which you're traveling. There are many signs along the way. What are they saying to you? Are the messages positive or negative? Are they warnings or affirmations? Picture the signs.

Who put up the signs? Did they come from you? Have other people imposed their signs on you? Maybe God has put up a sign or two. Take a moment to think about what the signs are saying to you.

Walk along that highway—the road that beckons you. Where is that road leading? Is God there with you or are you alone?

[Spend about 15-20 minutes in silence.]

FURTHER ON, DEEPER IN

Use the space below to share your own thoughts and reflections.

COMPANIONS ON THE JOURNEY

SILENCE IS GOD'S FIRST LANGUAGE; EVERYTHING ELSE IS A POOR TRANSLATION. IN ORDER TO HEAR THE LANGUAGE, WE MUST LEARN TO BE STILL AND TO REST IN GOD.

—THOMAS KEATING (BORN 1923), TRAPPIST MONK
INVITATION TO LOVE

DAY 3

LISTENING

Isaiah 6:1-8

1. In the year that King Uzziah died, I saw the Lord seated on a throne, high and exalted, and the train of his robe filled the temple.

2. Above him were seraphs, each with six wings: With two wings they covered their faces, with two they covered their feet, and with two they were flying.

3. And they were calling to one another: "Holy, holy, holy is the Lord Almighty; the whole earth is full of his glory."

4. At the sound of their voices the doorposts and thresholds shook and the temple was filled with smoke.

5. "Woe to me!" I cried. "I am ruined! For I am a man of unclean lips, and I live among a people of unclean lips, and my eyes have seen the King, the Lord Almighty."

6. Then one of the seraphs flew to me with a live coal in his hand, which he had taken with tongs from the altar.

7. With it he touched my mouth and said, "See, this has touched your lips; your guilt is taken away and your sin atoned for."

8. Then I heard the voice of the Lord saying, "Whom shall I send? And who will go for us?"
   And I said, *"Here am I. Send me!"*

MEDITATION

The words, "send me," seem simple enough. But how many amazing adventures, incredible journeys, and odysseys of faith have been launched by someone who, moved by a vision of God, said, "Send me"?

We live in a me-focused culture: "Give me." "Love me."

"Admire me." "Laugh at me." "Appreciate me." "Help me." "Notice me." "Send me" doesn't usually make the cut.

What me-phrases are filling your life today? Are they shaped by a vision of God (Isaiah 6:1), or are they rooted in the voices and images of the culture, your family, or your friends? Take a moment to jot down your thoughts.

[Pause to journal.]

Isaiah wrote, *"In the year that King Uzziah died,* I saw the Lord." Sometimes the me-phrases in our lives are shaped, not by the God who lives, but by someone or something that has died. Maybe it's a dream that disappeared, a relationship that ended badly, a self-image assassinated by cruelty, or a family strangled by divorce. Is that your story today? Listen quietly to the words, *"In the year that King Uzziah died,* I saw the Lord." Are you hearing God speak in your life?

Read this passage slowly again. Take note of the attributes of God Isaiah saw in his vision ("I saw the Lord seated on a throne, high and exalted, and the train of his robe filled the temple"; "my eyes have seen the King, the Lord Almighty").

The God of Isaiah was a God enthroned, high and lifted up, holy and mighty. When Isaiah saw God, his immediate thought was not, *Send me*, but *Woe to me* (verse 5).

As you look at your life today and think about the traffic jam of me-phrases congesting your soul and slowing you on the highway of God's call, perhaps the way to freedom is to change your "me" focus to a God focus. Admit to yourself: *Even if everybody I meet today loves me, admires me, laughs at me, and thinks I'm cool—even if all my dreams were still alive, my relationship was still going strong, my mom and dad were still together—without God's mighty touch, I would be in a desperate place still.* "Ruined" was the word used by Isaiah in verse 5.

As you read the verses one last time, slowly and prayerfully consider the me-phrases driving you, as well as the ones stalling you and stopping you. Think also about the God who calls you to a place of stunning discovery and obedient adventure.

Simple words. Real challenges. A huge vision.

What would it mean for you today to move from "*Love* me" to "Woe to me" to "Send me"?

FURTHER ON, DEEPER IN

Use the space below to share your own thoughts and reflections.

COMPANIONS ON THE JOURNEY

IN SCRIPTURE, GOD SPEAKS TO US, AND IN PRAYER, WE SPEAK TO GOD.

—ST. CYPRIAN, THIRD-CENTURY BISHOP AND MARTYR

DAY 4

LISTENING

Hebrews 4:12-16

12 For the word of God is living and active. Sharper than any double-edged sword, it penetrates even to dividing soul and spirit, joints and marrow; it judges the thoughts and attitudes of the heart.

13 Nothing in all creation is hidden from God's sight. *Everything is uncovered and laid bare before the eyes of him to whom we must give account.*

14 Therefore, since we have a great high priest who has gone through the heavens, Jesus the Son of God, let us hold firmly to the faith we profess.

15 For we do not have a high priest who is unable to sympathize with our weaknesses, but we have one who has been tempted in every way, just as we are—yet was without sin.

16 Let us then approach the throne of grace with confidence, so that we may receive mercy and find grace to help us in our time of need.

MEDITATION

Take time to quiet your mind and focus your heart. Take three deep breaths. Then slowly read the passage.

[Pause to read.]

Have you ever had a nightmare in which you're standing in front of a group of people giving a speech, and it occurs to you—funny you hadn't noticed it earlier—you're not wearing any clothes? It's a common dream of humiliation and shame, embarrassment and self-consciousness. One that points to an almost primal fear of exposure. All of us are afraid people will see us for who we are—frauds, fakers, phonies, and failures.

That's one reason we find it hard sometimes to read the Bible. It's like the preacher said: "The Bible won't keep you from sin, but sin will keep you from the Bible." Scripture is the probe, exposing the deepest places of our heart—"even to dividing soul and spirit, joints and marrow; it judges the thoughts and attitudes of the heart. Nothing in all creation is hidden from God's sight."

Begin your *lectio* exercise by reading slowly verses 12 and 13. Allow yourself time and space to consider prayerfully each phrase:

- "The Word of God...penetrates even to dividing soul and spirit..."

- "joints and marrow"

- "it judges the thoughts and attitudes of the heart..."

- "Nothing in all creation is hidden from God's sight."

- "Everything is uncovered and laid bare before the eyes of him to whom we must give account."

How does it feel to be under the probing point of a double-edged sword? Awkward? Scary? Unjust? Shameful? Humiliating? But what if the blade is not in the hands of an executioner who wants to condemn us, but instead in the hands of the great Physician who wants to save us?

Read slowly verse 15: "For we do not have a high priest who is unable to sympathize with our weaknesses, but we have one who has been tempted in every way, just as we are—yet was without sin." As you meditate on those words, pray them back to Jesus in praise. Don't rush. Ponder each phrase for a moment. You may want to journal some of your thoughts and feelings in the following space.

Jesus, you are not a high priest who is unable to sympathize with my weaknesses. You know how I struggle with fear, doubt, selfishness

Jesus, you have been tempted in every way, just as I have. Yet you were without sin. Maybe you didn't face the same exact circumstances, but you know what it's like to face as I have.

Now read verse 16: "Let us then approach the throne of grace with confidence, so that we may receive mercy and find grace to help us in our time of need."

Imagine yourself standing before the throne of God—naked and exposed, with all of your flaws apparent. Come before him now, not with fear and shame, but with confidence that the God of grace and mercy exposes us so we will give up our hiding. Take comfort in the fact he probes us so, like a surgeon, he might cut out the cancer of sin and make us whole.

Rest now in that place. Linger there. Approach God's throne, knowing God loves you as you are.

FURTHER ON, DEEPER IN:

Use the space below to share your own thoughts and reflections.

COMPANIONS ON THE JOURNEY

THE BIBLE WITHOUT THE HOLY SPIRIT IS A SUNDIAL BY MOONLIGHT.

—DWIGHT L. MOODY (1837-1899), U.S. EVANGELIST

DAY 5

LISTENING

Psalm 23:1-6

1 *The Lord is my shepherd, I shall not be in want.*

2 He makes me lie down in green pastures, he leads me beside quiet waters,

3 he restores my soul. He guides me in paths of righteousness for his name's sake.

4 Even though I walk through the valley of the shadow of death, I will fear no evil, for you are with me; your rod and your staff, they comfort me.

5 You prepare a table before me in the presence of my enemies. You anoint my head with oil; my cup overflows.

6 Surely goodness and love will follow me all the days of my life, and I will dwell in the house of the Lord forever.

MEDITATION

Believers throughout history have listened to God prayerfully by reading through the book of Psalms. As Israel's very first book of worship songs, it offers us the chance to embrace fellowship with God wherever we find ourselves. In good times and bad times. Times of anger and times of great joy. Times of hope and times of deep despair. Times of certainty and times of dark questioning. That's one of the reasons Christians for centuries have made a habit of praying the words of the Psalms.

For this experience of holy listening, you'll be reading Psalm 23 and meditating prayfully on each line. (For this exercise we are indebted to a friend, Andy Flannagan, an Irish singer-songwriter who lives in the U.K.)

As you quiet your mind, read the whole psalm. Then slowly read the following version, stopping to consider each word written between the lines. Breathe in slowly as you read each word and consider prayerfully how each gift of the Shepherd plays out in your own life.

The Lord is my shepherd, I shall not be in want.

Supply

He makes me lie down in green pastures,

Rest

he leads me beside quiet waters,

Refreshment

he restores my soul.

Healing

He guides me in paths of righteousness

Guidance

for his name's sake.

Purpose

Even though I walk through the valley of the shadow of death,

Challenge

I will fear no evil,

Assurance

for you are with me;

Faithfulness

your rod and your staff, they comfort me.

Comfort

You prepare a table before me in the presence of my enemies. You anoint my head with oil; my cup overflows.

Abundance

Surely goodness and love will follow me all the days of my life,

Blessing

and I will dwell in the house of the Lord forever.

Security

FURTHER ON, DEEPER IN

Use the space below to share your own thoughts and reflections.

I need to learn Your voice
to hear where You are calling
me to... Jesus please reveal
Yourself to me so I can know You.

COMPANIONS ON THE JOURNEY

THE MAN WHO ENTERS BY THE GATE IS THE SHEPHERD OF HIS SHEEP. THE WATCHMAN OPENS THE GATE FOR HIM, AND *THE SHEEP LISTEN TO HIS VOICE.* HE CALLS HIS OWN SHEEP BY NAME AND LEADS THEM OUT. WHEN HE HAS BROUGHT OUT ALL HIS OWN, HE GOES ON AHEAD OF THEM, AND HIS SHEEP FOLLOW HIM BECAUSE *THEY KNOW HIS VOICE.*

—JESUS, JOHN 10:2-4, NIV

DAY 6

LISTENING

John 13:1-5, 23

1 It was just before the Passover Feast. Jesus knew that the time had come for him to leave this world and go to the Father. *Having loved his own who were in the world, he now showed them the full extent of his love.*

2 The evening meal was being served, and the devil had already prompted Judas Iscariot, son of Simon, to betray Jesus.

3 Jesus knew that the Father had put all things under his power, and that he had come from God and was returning to God;

4 so he got up from the meal, took off his outer clothing, and wrapped a towel around his waist.

5 After that, he poured water into a basin and began to wash his disciples' feet, drying them with the towel that was wrapped around him....

23 One of them, the disciple whom Jesus loved, was reclining next to him.

MEDITATION

Imagine you're present at the Last Supper. The meal is over, and Jesus leans back to recline near the table, as was the custom of that time. He's among his disciples, people with whom he's shared three powerful, challenging years. They've all been through much together. Yet Jesus knows much is still yet to come. Imagine what the scene must have looked like.

Now imagine Jesus asks you to join him. What are you feeling as he calls you to him? Are you thrilled? Nervous?

Fearful? Contented? Do you feel safe or vulnerable—or perhaps a combination of both? Pay attention to your response and your emotions. Take a moment to figure them out. Then imagine Jesus invites you to lay your head on his chest. He's inviting you to listen to the very heart-beat of God. What's your response? As you listen, what do you hear?

[Spend about 15-20 minutes in silence.]

FURTHER ON, DEEPER IN

Use the space below to share your own thoughts and reflections.

COMPANIONS ON THE JOURNEY

SILENCE IS SOLITUDE PRACTICED IN ACTION....THE WORD OF GOD IS BORN OUT OF THE ETERNAL SILENCE OF GOD, AND IT IS TO THIS WORD OUT OF SILENCE THAT WE WANT TO BE WITNESSES.

—HENRI NOUWEN (1932-1996), CATHOLIC PRIEST AND AUTHOR
THE WAY OF THE HEART

DAY 7

afraid while God is trying to show him the answer ←

LISTENING

Exodus 4:1-5

1 Moses answered, "What if they do not believe me or listen to me and say, 'The Lord did not appear to you'?"

2 *Then the Lord said to him, "What is that in your hand?"*
"A staff," he replied.

3 *The Lord said, "Throw it on the ground."*
Moses threw it on the ground and it became a snake, and he ran from it.

4 *Then the Lord said to him, "Reach out your hand and take it by the tail." So Moses reached out and took hold of the snake and it turned back into a staff in his hand.*

5 "This," said the Lord, "is so that they may believe that the Lord, the God of their fathers—the God of Abraham, the God of Isaac and the God of Jacob—has appeared to you."

MEDITATION

Moses had been called by God to a task so radical, so huge, so impossible, it must have seemed outrageous. He was supposed to lead the Hebrew people out of slavery in Egypt and into a new land set aside by God.

But why Moses?

His past was less than great. His family situation was weird, to say the least (Exodus 2:1-10). He was a known murderer (Exodus 2:11-15). He was a fugitive on the run (Exodus 2:15).

His future didn't look promising, either. He was a fugitive *running back* to the scene of his crime (Exodus 3:10).

He had a lousy reputation (Exodus 4:1). And he was not very good at public speaking (Exodus 4:10).

Yet God said, "Go."

Read slowly, again, the first five verses of Exodus 4. What is Moses feeling? Is it something you've ever felt? Journal your thoughts and feelings in the following space.

[Pause to journal.]

Read the passage again, slowly. This time listen *for what God is saying.*

In the face of Moses' guilt and self doubt, God asks one odd question and gives two strange commands. The question is simply, "What is that in your hand?" Moses replies, "A staff." And God gives the first command: "Throw it on the ground." When the stick becomes a snake, God gives the second command: "Reach out your hand and take it by the tail."

Put yourself in Moses' position. You've spent the last 40 years tending sheep in the fields. You know from experience that a snake is dangerous, especially when it's grabbed by the tail and its head is left free to strike. What would you be thinking about God's command?

Perhaps God was giving Moses a vivid picture of how the things we fear—the memories and doubts that poison our future, that lie between us and where God wants us to go—need to be confronted head-on. Perhaps God was helping Moses understand the deep guilt, forgotten hopes, and lost dreams of the past can be either a snake on the ground intimidating you or, through his power and grace, a rod in the hand.

Maybe you're reading this passage with your own set

Moses had to give one command at a time, Doesn't know the whole plan yet, just how to follow what he does know

of fears, intimidations, painful memories, and deep regrets. If so, how have they stood between you and the journey to which <u>God is calling you?</u> → *to be his disciple*

And what is that in *your* hand?

is fear of not being loved

Maybe right now in the silence, through this passage, God is inviting you to throw down that stuff before him—to allow him to change the snake on the ground into a rod in your hand.

In the following space, write down some of the "snakes" that frighten or intimidate you, and listen quietly for God's word of forgiveness and assurance.

FURTHER ON, DEEPER IN

Use the space below to share your own thoughts and reflections.

- *fear of not being loved or liked if I radically live the gospel*
- *fear of not being happy w/ God's plan*
- *fear of missing out + others being happier than I am*

COMPANIONS ON THE JOURNEY

GOD IS NEARER TO US THAN WE ARE TO OURSELVES.

PAUL TILLICH (1886-1965), GERMAN THEOLOGIAN AND PROFESSOR
THE SHAKING OF THE FOUNDATIONS

DAY 8

LISTENING

Matthew 12:9-13

⁹ Going on from that place, he went into their synagogue,

¹⁰ and a man with a shriveled hand was there. Looking for a reason to accuse Jesus, they asked him, "Is it lawful to heal on the Sabbath?"

¹¹ He said to them, "If any of you has a sheep and it falls into a pit on the Sabbath, will you not take hold of it and lift it out?

¹² How much more valuable is a man than a sheep! Therefore it is lawful to do good on the Sabbath."

¹³ Then he said to the man, *"Stretch out your hand." So he stretched it out and it was completely restored, just as sound as the other.*

MEDITATION

Read this passage slowly two times. Try to experience it with your senses. *Feel* the closeness of the heat and the crowd packing the temple courts to watch the showdown. *Listen* for the angry voices of cynical, religious people watching and waiting for Jesus to commit the slightest infraction of Sabbath law so they could pounce on him with their accusations. *Smell* the lingering aroma of incense, still strong from the morning offering. And take a moment to *look* at the unnamed man in the middle of the crowd, on this stage of high drama, playing a role he'd never expected—a person Matthew describes only as "a man with a shriveled hand."

[Take time now to read this passage slowly. Remember, don't just read the words, experience them.]

For a few minutes, ponder this thought quietly: *You are the person with the shriveled hand. Your life is marked by a dry and lifeless limb. It wasn't always this way. Your hand used to be flush with blood and muscle. It used to be a hand you could feel with and touch with, a hand you could reach out to offer help or love, a hand you could flex and use for work. But now it hangs at your side, a constant symbol of shame, disappointment, and disability.*

What do you feel when you read these words: *shame, disappointment, disability?* Do they take you to any places of dryness and pain in your own life? Maybe you've found yourself in a place where your own capacity to touch and feel has grown limp with discouragement. Maybe you were in church or youth group, but you could feel it—the hands that used to be lifted up in worship remained at your side, dangling and lifeless? Listen here intently to what God might say to you. Journal your thoughts in the following space.

[Pause to journal.]

It may seem like a really bad idea to expose your dryness right in the middle of the church, surrounded by religious people. But that day in the temple, Jesus gave the man a simple command: "Stretch out your hand." In other words, Jesus said, "Expose to me your places of dryness and weakness, your symptoms of lifelessness and loss, so I can make you whole." What a stunning invitation! What a scandal of grace! What a picture of divine love! To God we are not props or object lessons about Sabbath law. We are his precious property, the objects of his deep affection.

Listen again to Jesus' words in verse 12:

"If any of you has a sheep and it falls into a pit on the

Sabbath, will you not take hold of it and lift it out? How much more valuable is a man than a sheep! Therefore it is lawful to do good on the Sabbath."

Before you close this time of meditation, imagine for a few minutes Jesus saying to you, "Stretch out your hand. Stretch out your dryness. Stretch out your shame before me, so I can make you whole. You are valuable to me." Journal your reflections in the following space.

FURTHER ON, DEEPER IN

Use the space below to share your own thoughts and reflections.

COMPANIONS ON THE JOURNEY

QUIETUDE, WHICH SOME MEN CANNOT ABIDE BECAUSE IT REVEALS THEIR INWARD POVERTY, IS AS A PALACE OF CEDAR TO THE WISE, FOR ALONG ITS HALLOWED COURTS THE KING IN HIS BEAUTY DEIGNS TO WALK.

—CHARLES HADDON SPURGEON (1834-1892), BAPTIST PASTOR CITED IN *PATCHES OF GODLIGHT* BY JAN KARON

DAY 9

LISTENING

Isaiah 43:15-21

15 "I am the Lord, your Holy One, Israel's Creator, your King."

16 This is what the Lord says— he who made a way through the sea, a path through the mighty waters,

17 who drew out the chariots and horses, the army and reinforcements together, and they lay there, never to rise again, extinguished, snuffed out like a wick:

18 *"Forget the former things; do not dwell on the past.*

19 *See, I am doing a new thing! Now it springs up; do you not perceive it?* I am making a way in the desert and streams in the wasteland.

20 The wild animals honor me, the jackals and the owls, because I provide water in the desert and streams in the wasteland, to give drink to my people, my chosen,

21 the people I formed for myself that they may proclaim my praise.

MEDITATION:

God's promise is to make a way in the desert and streams in the wasteland. God promises something new will spring forth from a place dried up by something old. He encourages you to dwell not on your past but on the now and the new.

Unfortunately sometimes our past makes it tough to focus on the present. Are there memories of disappointment, disobedience, betrayal, or regret distracting you from the new things God wishes to do in your life? If so, jot down some of those pieces of your past.

Now imagine a dry, barren wasteland being transformed by fresh streams of water. Imagine your life being irrigated by God's overflowing love and grace. Don't move too quickly over this image. Close your eyes for a moment, if it helps, and imagine grace and mercy washing, flowing, splashing over parched, dried-up memories. What might spring forth from a life so refreshed? That's the mystery and wonder of your present.

Imagine you and God are standing together, looking over a field, a place that once was a desert, but now is sprinkled with greenery and growth. Maybe that growth is still in its earliest stages. The point is it's alive with new hope. In the following space, write what you think God might say to you as the two of you look across the landscape of your life today. What would he invite you to see?

FURTHER ON, DEEPER IN

Use the space below and on the following page to share your own thoughts and reflections.

COMPANIONS ON THE JOURNEY

SURPRISE ME, LORD, AS A SEED SURPRISES ITSELF.

—GEORGE HERBERT (1593-1633), ENGLISH POET

DAY 10

LISTENING

Jeremiah 3:11-22

[11] The Lord said to me...

[12] *"Go, proclaim this message toward the north:*
" 'Return, faithless Israel,' declares the Lord, 'I will frown on you no longer, for I am merciful,' declares the Lord, 'I will not be angry forever.

[13] *Only acknowledge your guilt*—you have rebelled against the Lord your God, you have scattered your favors to foreign gods under every spreading tree, and have not obeyed me,' " declares the Lord.

[14] "Return, faithless people," declares the Lord, "for I am your husband. I will choose you—one from a town and two from a clan—and bring you to Zion.

[15] Then I will give you shepherds after my own heart, who will lead you with knowledge and understanding.

[16] In those days, when your numbers have increased greatly in the land," declares the Lord, "men will no longer say, 'The ark of the covenant of the Lord.' It will never enter their minds or be remembered; it will not be missed, nor will another one be made.

[17] At that time they will call Jerusalem The Throne of the Lord, and all nations will gather in Jerusalem to honor the name of the Lord. No longer will they follow the stubbornness of their evil hearts.

[18] In those days the house of Judah will join the house of Israel, and together they will come from a northern land to the land I gave your forefathers as an inheritance.

[19] "I myself said,
" 'How gladly would I treat you like sons and give you a desirable land, the most beautiful inheritance of any nation.' I thought you would call me 'Father' and not turn away from following me.

²⁰ But like a woman unfaithful to her husband, so you have been unfaithful to me, O house of Israel," declares the Lord.

²¹ A cry is heard on the barren heights, the weeping and pleading of the people of Israel, because they have perverted their ways and have forgotten the Lord their God.

²² "Return, faithless people; I will cure you of backsliding."

MEDITATION

Read these verses two times, slowly and prayerfully. Listen carefully. Is there a portion of this passage tugging at your heart in a particular way?

How do you feel when you read the words, "'But like a woman unfaithful to her husband, so you have been unfaithful to me, O house of Israel,' declares the Lord." Is there any sense, today, in which you might be hearing God speak these words to you?

Think about a time when you were unfaithful to God. Don't hurry past this memory. Recall what brought you to that place. What was it that made you turn away from God? Why did that event, that situation, that set of circumstances, that person make you turn away from the God who chose you as his own?

You may want to stop and sit silently to think about that question. Try to remember the failure, guilt, or disappointment you felt when you realized you'd let God down. Take a few moments to record your thoughts and feelings in the following space.

[Pause to journal.]

Read the passage a third time, listening especially to God's word of invitation to you in verses 12 and 13.

"'Return, faithless Israel,' declares the Lord, 'I will frown on you no longer, for I am merciful,' declares the Lord, 'I will not be angry forever. Only acknowledge your guilt—you have rebelled against the Lord your God, you have scattered your favors to foreign gods under every spreading tree, and have not obeyed me,'" declares the Lord.

How does it make you feel to realize no matter how much you deny him and rebel against him, God still calls you back to his side? Unworthy? Unwelcome? Ungrateful? Or do you feel loved unconditionally?

God will not be angry forever. He is merciful.

"Only acknowledge your guilt—you have rebelled against the Lord your God" (verse 13).

God knows where you've been. He knows what you've done. He knows everything. Yet he says, "Come back!"

In the following space, where earlier you recorded your feelings about failure, disappointment, or guilt, write in big letters over everything you've written, "Return to me."

FURTHER ON, DEEPER IN

Use the space below and on the following page to share your own thoughts and reflections.

COMPANIONS ON THE JOURNEY

TOO MANY OF US PANIC IN THE DARK. WE DON'T UNDERSTAND THAT IT'S
A HOLY DARK AND THAT THE IDEA IS TO SURRENDER TO IT AND JOURNEY
THROUGH TO REAL LIGHT.

SUE MONK KIDD (BORN 1948), U.S. AUTHOR AND NURSE
CITED IN *LITTLE PIECES OF LIGHT* BY JOYCE RUPP

DAY 11

LISTENING

Jeremiah 23:16-24

16 This is what the Lord Almighty says:
"Do not listen to what the prophets are prophesying to you; they fill you with false hopes. They speak visions from their own minds, not from the mouth of the Lord.

17 They keep saying to those who despise me, 'The Lord says: You will have peace.' And to all who follow the stubbornness of their hearts they say, 'No harm will come to you.'

18 But which of them has stood in the council of the Lord to see or to hear his word? Who has listened and heard his word?

19 See, the storm of the Lord will burst out in wrath, a whirlwind swirling down on the heads of the wicked.

20 The anger of the Lord will not turn back until he fully accomplishes the purposes of his heart. In days to come you will understand it clearly.

21 I did not send these prophets, yet they have run with their message; I did not speak to them, yet they have prophesied.

22 But if they had stood in my council, they would have proclaimed my words to my people and would have turned them from their evil ways and from their evil deeds.

23 *"Am I only a God nearby," declares the Lord, "and not a God far away?*

24 *Can anyone hide in secret places so that I cannot see him?" declares the Lord.* "Do not I fill heaven and earth?" declares the Lord.

MEDITATION

Read slowly the words spoken by God in verse 23: "Am I only a God nearby, and not a God far away?"

For a few minutes, dwell on the phrase, "a God nearby." What sorts of feelings do those words provoke in you? Perhaps they serve as words of encouragement, words of comfort, or words of reassurance. Perhaps you find them hard to believe. Perhaps you hear them as words of warning (see verse 24). Journal your feelings in the space on the following page.

Now move on to the phrase, "a God far away." What sort of words, images, and feelings are provoked by that phrase? Do you find reassurance in those words? Or do they seem more like words of departure, dismissal, distance, and separation?

Which of the two concepts represents best what you feel right now: the God who is near or the God who is far away? Saint Ignatius, a Jesuit priest, described the life of faith as a life of two tides, consolation and desolation. Consolation is made up of "God near" times—times when God feels present, when we're consoled by his nearness, when the waves of his presence seem to wash up around us. But there are also times in the life of faith when the tide goes out—times of desolation, times when God seems far away.

As you think about these two tides, consolation and desolation, imagine God is an ocean, immense in his presence, awesome in his depths, unfathomable in his mysteries. If it helps, close your eyes for a moment to visualize the waves coming in and going out.

Now here's the amazing part: Today, whether the tide is in or out, whether God seems near or far away, he is close at hand. Whether you feel the rush of the waves under your feet ("the God nearby"), or the horizons of the beachfront seem to stretch well out from shore ("the God far away"), *you are still on the shoreline of his presence.* And what he desires, through the high tides of nearness and low tides of distance, is that you draw closer to him.

Close your time of meditation by allowing yourself to be drawn closer to the God near/God far away.

FURTHER ON, DEEPER IN

Use the space below to share your own thoughts and reflections.

COMPANIONS ON THE JOURNEY

ALWAYS BE IN A STATE OF EXPECTANCY, AND SEE THAT YOU LEAVE ROOM FOR GOD TO COME IN AS HE LIKES.

—OSWALD CHAMBERS (1874-1917), CHRISTIAN WRITER
MY UTMOST FOR HIS HIGHEST

DAY 12

LISTENING

Exodus 3:1-6

¹   Now Moses was tending the flock of Jethro his father-in-law, the priest of Midian, and he led the flock to the far side of the desert and came to Horeb, the mountain of God.

²   *There the angel of the Lord appeared to him in flames of fire from within a bush. Moses saw that though the bush was on fire it did not burn up.*

³   *So Moses thought, "I will go over and see this strange sight— why the bush does not burn up."*

⁴   When the Lord saw that he had gone over to look, God called to him from within the bush, "Moses! Moses!" And Moses said, "Here I am."

⁵   "Do not come any closer," God said. "Take off your sandals, for the place where you are standing is holy ground."

⁶   Then he said, "I am the God of your father, the God of Abraham, the God of Isaac and the God of Jacob."

MEDITATION

Think about what God's startling appearance must have been like for Moses. Imagine how you might have felt if you'd been in Moses' sandals. In the following space, jot down your thoughts about what Moses might have written in his own journal at the end of his phenomenal day.

Think back on your own life over the past 24 hours. Were you able to hear God or see his presence in your life? If so, how and when did that happen? Write down your thoughts as you look back on your day. Remember, even though the bushes you saw today were relatively smoke-free, sometimes God speaks to us in less dramatic ways. If you did hear God, how did he speak to you? How did you respond? What kind of protests did you offer? What is God's word of encouragement for you today?

Remember, too, even if you can't think of a time when you saw or heard God today, that doesn't mean God was silent or absent. If you didn't hear or sense God's presence in your life today, relax. Your very attention right now in reading these words is a clear indication you're willing to listen. And that's a gift to God.

FURTHER ON, DEEPER IN

Use the space below to share your own thoughts and reflections.

COMPANIONS ON THE JOURNEY

EARTH'S CRAMMED WITH HEAVEN, AND EVERY COMMON BUSH AFIRE WITH GOD; AND ONLY HE WHO SEES TAKES OFF HIS SHOES; THE REST SIT ROUND IT AND PLUCK BLACKBERRIES.

—ELIZABETH BARRETT BROWNING (1806-1861), ENGLISH POET
AURORA LEIGH. BOOK VII.

DAY 13

LISTENING

Psalm 46:1-11

1　God is our refuge and strength, an ever-present help in trouble.

2　Therefore we will not fear, though the earth give way and the mountains fall into the heart of the sea,

3　though its waters roar and foam and the mountains quake with their surging.　　　　　*Selah*

4　There is a river whose streams make glad the city of God, the holy place where the Most High dwells.

5　God is within her, she will not fall; God will help her at break of day.

6　Nations are in uproar, kingdoms fall; he lifts his voice, the earth melts.

7　The Lord Almighty is with us; the God of Jacob is our fortress.　　　　　*Selah*

8　Come and see the works of the Lord, the desolations he has brought on the earth.

9　He makes wars cease to the ends of the earth; he breaks the bow and shatters the spear, he burns the shields with fire.

10　*"Be still, and know that I am God; I will be exalted among the nations,* I will be exalted in the earth."

11　The Lord Almighty is with us; the God of Jacob is our fortress.　　　　　*Selah*

MEDITATION

Where were you on September 11, 2001, at 8:46 a.m.? How many times did you have to see the images of those planes flying into the twin towers of New York City's World Trade Center before you were able to believe it was really happening?

What about the morning of December 26, 2004? Do you remember how you felt when you heard the reports of the tsunami that broke across the Indian Ocean, leaving in its wake a staggering death toll and unimaginable devastation?

From time to time, we hear some leader or official talk about "life returning to normal," and we can't help but wonder: *What does "normal" look like in a world filled with such violence, pain, and human tragedy?*

Maybe our fundamental problem is that our "old normal" is defined by unreality—the notion that somehow we might have wealth enough, or education enough, or power enough to make ourselves secure from the world's violence and uncertainty.

The message of Psalm 46 is stark and realistic. We live in a world marked by violence and upheaval, including

- the violence of nature—earthquakes, volcanoes, floods (verses 1-3)

- the violence of geopolitical turmoil (verse 6)

- the violence of war (verse 9)

Sometimes it feels as though the world is coming apart. Maybe it's global turmoil far away. Maybe it's personal turmoil, as close as your everyday life.

In the midst of it all, the psalmist reveals God's work for us: "Be still, and know that I am God."

What if God were to speak those words to you personally today? What if he were to bend down close, put his hands on your face, look you in the eye, call you by name, and whisper with that still, small voice, "Be still, and know that I am God"?

Listen to that voice and, in the following space, write out your reflections as you hear God say those words to you.

FURTHER ON, DEEPER IN

Use the space below to share your own thoughts and reflections.

"Be still..."

"and know..."

"that I am God."

COMPANIONS ON THE JOURNEY

BLESSED IS THE MAN WHOSE IMAGINATION *STOPS* WITH GOD.

—ROY PUTNAM, 20TH CENTURY METHODIST PASTOR

DAY 14

LISTENING

Luke 13:11-13

11 And a woman was there who had been crippled by a spirit for eighteen years. *She was bent over and could not straighten up at all.*

12 When Jesus saw her, he called her forward and said to her, "Woman, you are set free from your infirmity."

13 Then he put his hands on her, and immediately she straightened up and praised God.

MEDITATION

What if *you* were the woman "crippled by a spirit for eighteen years"? Imagine for the last eighteen years of your life, your entire horizon ended about a yard in front of your feet. Your experience of a sunset doesn't involve splashing colors, but growing shadows. Your relationships are marked not by smiles and eye contact, but by the sound of a voice and the sight of familiar feet. What would it be like to spend all day, every day, staring at the ground? What if you could never look up?

In the following space jot down some of the ways your life would be different if you spent the next 24 hours bent over. Think about sights you wouldn't see—a friend's smile, the sunset, your computer screen. Relationships you couldn't enjoy fully. Activities you couldn't possibly do.

If you were unable to straighten up at all, how would your life be "crippled"? Close your eyes for a few moments to imagine what that might be like. Then jot down your responses.

[Pause to journal.]

Now imagine what it might be like to encounter Jesus. You can't look into his face. You can see only his sandals. But after all the years of being unable to look up, your sense of touch is heightened. You feel on your head the strong, wide hand of a carpenter. Likewise, your hearing, sensitized by years of sightlessness, is alerted by the sound of a voice, gentle and confident: "You are set free from your infirmity."

What a stunning reversal—from stooped over to standing straight, from pleading for mercy to praising for grace.

Quietly ponder this passage for a few minutes. Read it a few times. Then ask yourself, "How does this woman's story mirror my own?" Write your reflections in the following space.

FURTHER ON, DEEPER IN

Use the space below and on the following page to share your own thoughts and reflections.

COMPANIONS ON THE JOURNEY

BY THE READING OF SCRIPTURE I AM SO RENEWED THAT ALL NATURE
SEEMS RENEWED AROUND ME AND WITH ME. THE SKY SEEMS TO BE
PURER, A COOLER BLUE, THE TREES A DEEPER GREEN, LIGHT IS SHARPER
ON THE OUTLINES OF THE FOREST AND THE HILLS, AND THE WHOLE WORLD
IS CHARGED WITH THE GLORY OF GOD AND I FIND FIRE AND MUSIC IN THE
EARTH UNDER MY FEET.

—THOMAS MERTON (1915-1968), TRAPPIST MONK
CITED IN *LECTIO DIVINA* BY M. BASIL PENNINGTON

DAY 15

LISTENING

Jeremiah 31:31-34

³¹ "The time is coming," declares the Lord, "when I will make a new covenant with the house of Israel and with the house of Judah.

³² It will not be like the covenant I made with their forefathers when I took them by the hand to lead them out of Egypt, because they broke my covenant, though I was a husband to them," declares the Lord.

³³ "This is the covenant I will make with the house of Israel after that time," declares the Lord. "I will put my law in their minds and write it on their hearts. I will be their God, and they will be my people.

³⁴ No longer will a man teach his neighbor, or a man his brother, saying, 'Know the Lord,' because they will all know me, from the least of them to the greatest," declares the Lord. *"For I will forgive their wickedness and will remember their sins no more."*

MEDITATION

[Note: Before you begin this exercise, see if you can find some wrapping paper. Don't take a long time to look for it. But if you can get your hands on some, it might help to make this exercise a little more vivid.]

Read the passage twice and take special notice of these words: "For I will forgive their wickedness and will remember their sins no more." It's an amazing phrase to consider. The God who is *omniscient*—the One who knows all—decides to forget some of the stuff he knows. It's the reverse of what most of us are used to. We have to *intend to remember* something, or we'll forget it. God has to *intend to forget something*, or he'll remember it! But that's the great news at the heart of this new covenant: God promises to remember our sins no more.

Take a few minutes right now to contemplate that notion, to unpack that gift. Don't rip it open and just start working through the rest of the exercise. Read it slowly, as if you are unfolding the wrapping paper around a precious gift.

[Pause to read.]

What are some of the things in your life you hope God might forget? Choices you've made? Places you've stepped backward, when you feel God called you to step forward? Words you've spoken that you can't take back? Shameful memories of failure, weakness, or unfaithfulness? Mull them over in your mind. Look at them. Name them. If you have the wrapping paper, take time to write your memories on the blank side of the paper. If not, use a piece of scrap paper or write them down in the following journaling section. Don't rush too quickly through this exercise. Whether the sins are small or large...whether they involve other people or just you...whether they were committed long ago or just this morning, write them down.

[Pause to write.]

The Greek word for *confession* is *homologeo*. Literally, it means *to say the same thing*. When we confess our sins, we name them, we write down, we speak them. We are saying, "God, I know you think of this as sin. I want you to know I do as well. This wasn't somebody else's fault or a little slip or 'just me being me.' This was *me* trying to be *you*—trying to be god of my own life, maker of my own rules. And that's sin." When we write down our sins, it's an act of confession.

It's also an act that opens the floodgates of God's forgiveness. "If we confess our sins," 1 John 1:9 reminds us, "he is faithful and just and will forgive us our sins and purify us from all unrighteousness."

The great news of the new covenant introduced in Jeremiah 31 is God chose to forget and forgive our sin. We praise him because he knows, because he rules, because he judges, because he loves, because he is, and because... he forgets! Imagine that.

As the final part of your confession, take the paper on which you've written your sins and tear it up. You may have to be a little creative if you wrote your sins in this book, but feel free to tear out the page. (If you don't want to rip the page from the book, write the words "Forgiven and Forgotten" over your sins until you can no longer read them.)

With those shreds of paper in your hand, spend some time in silence at the foot of God's throne. Then pray back your response, remembering God's great words of promise in Jeremiah 31.

"I will make a new covenant."

"I will put my law in their minds and write it on their hearts."

"I will be their God, and they will be my people."

"I will forgive their wickedness."

"I will remember their sins no more."

FURTHER ON, DEEPER IN

Use the space below to share your own thoughts and reflections.

COMPANIONS ON THE JOURNEY

"IT IS NEVER TOO LATE TO BE WHAT YOU MIGHT HAVE BEEN!"

—GEORGE ELIOT, A.K.A. MARY ANN EVANS (1819-1880), ENGLISH NOVELIST

DAY 16

LISTENING

Philippians 3:7-14

7 *But whatever was to my profit I now consider loss for the sake of Christ.*

8 What is more, I consider everything a loss compared to the surpassing greatness of knowing Christ Jesus my Lord, for whose sake I have lost all things. I consider them rubbish, that I may gain Christ

9 and be found in him, not having a righteousness of my own that comes from the law, but that which is through faith in Christ—the righteousness that comes from God and is by faith.

10 I want to know Christ and the power of his resurrection and the fellowship of sharing in his sufferings, becoming like him in his death,

11 and so, somehow, to attain to the resurrection from the dead.

12 Not that I have already obtained all this, or have already been made perfect, but I press on to take hold of that for which Christ Jesus took hold of me.

13 Brothers, I do not consider myself yet to have taken hold of it. But one thing I do: Forgetting what is behind and straining toward what is ahead,

14 I press on toward the goal to win the prize for which God has called me heavenward in Christ Jesus.

MEDITATION

This may be a difficult question, but think about it quietly for a few minutes: What have you *lost* for the sake of knowing Christ? What was to your *profit* that you now consider loss for the sake of Christ? Was it a circle of friends pulling you away from God? Was it a relationship holding you back? Was it family harmony and understanding? Were there habits, ways of spending free time, or other patterns of behavior that just didn't seem to fit with your desire to grow in Christ?

Sometimes, in an effort to make the life of faith more appealing, Christians gloss over the losses and consider only the gains. But the Christian life is, in reality, a mixture of both. The contemplative Christian writer Ignatius referred to this as a rhythm of desolation (loss) and consolation (gain). Granted, the gains far outweigh and surpass the losses, but both are real. And we're likely to feel them both vividly.

The apostle Paul is very honest about this aspect of knowing Christ. Listen to the words he uses in verses 7 and 8: *loss* (twice), *lost*, and *rubbish*. Those are words of desolation.

Close your eyes for a few minutes and consider the word loss ("Whatever was to my profit I now consider loss for the sake of Christ"). How does that loss feel to you? What does it mean for you in terms of your relationship with Jesus? Journal your thoughts in the following space.

[Pause to write your thoughts.]

If Paul were sitting with you right now, he would want you to know this passage is not just about loss; it's also about gain. This is the message of consolation: "I consider everything a loss compared to the surpassing greatness of knowing Christ Jesus my Lord, for whose sake I have lost all things. I consider them rubbish, *that I may gain Christ and be found in him*" (verses 8-9).

Take a few minutes to meditate on the phrase, "that I may gain Christ and be found in him." What does it mean for you personally to gain Christ? What have you gained through knowing Christ and being found in him? Try to move beyond Sunday school language here. Be specific. How has gaining Christ impacted your relationships, your perspective in life, your hopes, your fears, or your desires?

As you think through this question, it might be helpful to meditate on the phrase, "found in him." That's a pretty powerful image. Where do you find yourself "in him" right now? Are you at his feet, at his side, in his arms, in his lap? Do you feel the consolation there? Take a few moments to linger in that place. Journal your thoughts in the following space.

[Pause to write your thoughts.]

Read the words you've written one more time—words of desolation and words of consolation. Pray Paul's words in verses 7-9 as you finish your meditation on this passage.

FURTHER ON, DEEPER IN

Use the space below and on the following page to share your own thoughts and reflections.

COMPANIONS ON THE JOURNEY

WHEN WE CANNOT REASON DISCURSIVELY OR MAKE ACTS OF THE WILL WITH ANY SATISFACTION DURING PRAYER, ONE SHOULD GIVE THE SITUATION A QUIET WELCOME. ONE WILL BEGIN TO FEEL PEACE, TRANQUILITY, AND STRENGTH BECAUSE GOD IS NOW FEEDING THE SOUL DIRECTLY, GIVING HIS GRACE TO THE WILL ALONE AND ATTRACTING IT MYSTERIOUSLY TO HIMSELF.

—JOHN OF THE CROSS (1542-1591), CARMELITE MONK
THE LIVING FLAME OF LOVE

DAY 17

LISTENING

1 Samuel 7:5-13

5 Then Samuel said, "Assemble all Israel at Mizpah and I will intercede with the Lord for you."

6 When they had assembled at Mizpah, they drew water and poured it out before the Lord. On that day they fasted and there they confessed, "We have sinned against the Lord." And Samuel was leader of Israel at Mizpah.

7 When the Philistines heard that Israel had assembled at Mizpah, the rulers of the Philistines came up to attack them. And when the Israelites heard of it, they were afraid because of the Philistines.

8 They said to Samuel, "Do not stop crying out to the Lord our God for us, that he may rescue us from the hand of the Philistines."

9 Then Samuel took a suckling lamb and offered it up as a whole burnt offering to the Lord. He cried out to the Lord on Israel's behalf, and the Lord answered him.

10 While Samuel was sacrificing the burnt offering, the Philistines drew near to engage Israel in battle. But that day the Lord thundered with loud thunder against the Philistines and threw them into such a panic that they were routed before the Israelites.

11 The men of Israel rushed out of Mizpah and pursued the Philistines, slaughtering them along the way to a point below Beth Car.

12 *Then Samuel took a stone and set it up between Mizpah and Shen. He named it Ebenezer, saying, "Thus far has the Lord helped us."*

13 So the Philistines were subdued and did not invade Israelite territory again.

Throughout Samuel's lifetime, the hand of the Lord was against the Philistines.

MEDITATION

In the Old Testament, the Israelites sometimes placed a large stone or built a monument to mark where God had done a great work. Those monuments helped them remember God is faithful. The monuments were often given names, as in this story, where Samuel names the spot *Ebenezer,* which means literally "stone of help."

Think of the moments when God has done great works in your life. In what ways do these experiences serve as monuments to remind you of God's ongoing work in your life?

Think about one of these moments. Did it occur on a retreat or at a camp? Perhaps at a worship service? Did it happen at a really good place in your life? Or did it happen during a really hard time? Name that moment and ponder it for a while.

As you look back at your "Ebenezer" moment, consider what you learned about God in that place. In what ways did God help you in that time? If there were a plaque with an inscription on that monument, what would it say?

In your time of reflection, take that moment and set it up before God as a stone that marks his presence in your life saying, "Thus far has the Lord helped me."

FURTHER ON, DEEPER IN

Use the space below to share your own thoughts and reflections.

COMPANIONS ON THE JOURNEY

ONE ACT OF THANKSGIVING MADE WHEN THINGS GO WRONG IS WORTH A
THOUSAND WHEN THINGS GO WELL.

—ST. JOHN OF AVILA (1500-1569), SPANISH CATHOLIC PRIEST
AND THEOLOGIAN

DAY 18

LISTENING

James 1:2-8, 12

2   *Consider* it pure joy, my brothers, whenever you face trials of many kinds,

3   because you *know* that the testing of your faith develops perseverance.

4   Perseverance must finish its work so that you may be mature and complete, not lacking anything.

5   If any of you lacks wisdom, he should *ask* God, who gives generously to all without finding fault, and it will be given to him.

6   But when he asks, he must believe and not doubt, because he who doubts is like a wave of the sea, blown and tossed by the wind.

7   That man should not think he will receive anything from the Lord;

8   he is a double-minded man, unstable in all he does....

12 *Blessed* is the man who perseveres under trial, because when he has stood the test, he will receive the crown of life that God has promised to those who love him.

MEDITATION

Before you read this passage, take a minute to think about how you respond to disappointment. How do you deal with tough times—times when you think, *My life stinks. I'm going back to bed. Maybe I'll wake up for my senior year?*

Before you begin this meditation exercise, use the following space to write down some of the tough times, tough issues, tough questions, or tough relationships that make you feel as though you'd be better off if you'd stayed in bed.

[Pause to journal.]

Now slowly read the passage two times. As you read it, take special note of the italicized words.

[Pause to read the passage.]

The words *consider, know, ask,* and *blessed* mark a path that can lead us through the thick brush and undergrowth of tough times. The first steps—perhaps unsteady and a little unsure—begin with thoughtful reflection: *"Consider* it pure joy." Then, with the light of what we've seen, we gain the confidence to walk with a steadier step by the light of what we *know.* This gives us the confidence to *ask* for direction in those places where the trail is hard to read—or where it's easy to read but hard to walk. Finally we come to a clearing, the place where, at least for a few steps, the journey starts to make sense (*"Blessed* is the man who perseveres under trial").

Read the passage one more time. This time think about the journey of your own life—uphill and downhill, good times and bad times, times of clearing and times of confusion. As you read the words, pause to listen and reflect on your walk with God. Jot down your thoughts as you listen and pray.

FURTHER ON, DEEPER IN

Use the space below to share your own thoughts and reflections.

"Consider it pure joy, my brothers, whenever you face trials of many kinds..." (verse 2)

"because you *know* that the testing of your faith develops perseverance." (verse 3)

"If any of you lacks wisdom, he should *ask* God, who gives generously to all without finding fault, and it will be given to him." (verse 5)

"*Blessed* is the man who perseveres under trial, because when he has stood the test, he will receive the crown of life that God has promised to those who love him." (verse 12)

COMPANIONS ON THE JOURNEY

WE NEED THE PRAYERS OF WORDS, YES: THE WORDS ARE THE PATH TO CONTEMPLATION; BUT THE DEEPEST COMMUNION WITH GOD IS BEYOND WORDS, ON THE OTHER SIDE OF SILENCE.

—MADELEINE L'ENGLE (BORN 1918), U.S. NOVELIST
WALKING ON WATER

DAY 19

LISTENING

Genesis 22:1-14

1   Some time later God tested Abraham. He said to him, "Abraham!" "Here I am," he replied.

2   Then God said, "Take your son, your only son, Isaac, whom you love, and go to the region of Moriah. Sacrifice him there as a burnt offering on one of the mountains I will tell you about."

3   Early the next morning Abraham got up and saddled his donkey. He took with him two of his servants and his son Isaac. When he had cut enough wood for the burnt offering, he set out for the place God had told him about.

4   On the third day Abraham looked up and saw the place in the distance.

5   He said to his servants, "Stay here with the donkey while I and the boy go over there. We will worship and then we will come back to you."

6   Abraham took the wood for the burnt offering and placed it on his son Isaac, and he himself carried the fire and the knife. As the two of them went on together,

7   Isaac spoke up and said to his father Abraham, "Father?"
    "Yes, my son?" Abraham replied.
    "The fire and wood are here," Isaac said, "but where is the lamb for the burnt offering?"

8   Abraham answered, "God himself will provide the lamb for the burnt offering, my son." And the two of them went on together.

9   *When they reached the place God had told him about, Abraham built an altar there and arranged the wood on it. He bound his son Isaac and laid him on the altar, on top of the wood.*

¹⁰ *Then he reached out his hand and took the knife to slay his son.*

¹¹ *But the angel of the Lord called out to him from heaven, "Abraham! Abraham!"*

"Here I am," he replied.

¹² *"Do not lay a hand on the boy," he said. "Do not do anything to him. Now I know that you fear God, because you have not withheld from me your son, your only son."*

¹³ Abraham looked up and there in a thicket he saw a ram caught by its horns. He went over and took the ram and sacrificed it as a burnt offering instead of his son.

¹⁴ So Abraham called that place The Lord Will Provide. And to this day it is said, "On the mountain of the Lord it will be provided."

MEDITATION

As you read this poignant account of commitment and faithfulness, imagine yourself as Abraham facing the very real possibility of having to sacrifice your son—your *only* son, a son you love very much. Read again, very slowly, those fourteen verses trying to visualize the scene that day. Look closely at the physical landscape of the mountains of Moriah, as well as the mental landscape of Abraham as he contemplates the awful truth of what he is about to do. Remember, we know how this story ends. That day on the mountain Abraham had no way of knowing.

As Abraham, you're not sure which causes you greater pain: the sound of your son's voice asking where the lamb for sacrifice is or the sight of the sticks piled together in preparation for the fire. What are you feeling as you make your final preparations? What are your thoughts about God? What moves you to obey—or disobey—in the face of such sacrifice? Take a moment to journal some of your thoughts.

[Pause to journal.]

Now read what you've written. Do any of those thoughts and feelings describe some of what you feel now in *your* relationship with God? Is there something (or someone) precious to you that God might be asking you to give up as part of your love for him?

Imagine as you finish this meditation, you're building the fire for such a commitment. What is God's word to you as you meet him today on your Mount Moriah? Listen carefully. Stay in that place of anguish and uncertainty, even though it may be very uncomfortable. Remember, this isn't really a story about Abraham providing an offering; it's a story about God offering a provision.

So often, when we think of obedience, we think in terms of giving in, giving up, or just giving more. And, no doubt, there will be times when your obedient response to God will require you to sacrifice. But the drama of Mount Moriah reminds us God always gives more than he requires (that's grace), and his provision is always bigger than our offering.

FURTHER ON, DEEPER IN

Use the space below and on the following page to share your own thoughts and reflections.

COMPANIONS ON THE JOURNEY

BUT SUDDENLY WHAT HAD BEEN AN IDEAL HAD BECOME A DEMAND:
TOTAL SURRENDER TO GOD, THE ABSOLUTE LEAP IN THE DARK. THE
DEMAND WAS NOT EVEN "ALL OR NOTHING"...THAT STAGE HAD BEEN
PASSED. NOW, THE DEMAND WAS SIMPLY "ALL!"

—C. S. LEWIS (1898-1963), ENGLISH AUTHOR AND SCHOLAR
SURPRISED BY JOY

DAY 20

LISTENING

Luke 22:54-62

⁵⁴ Then seizing him, they led him away and took him into the house of the high priest. Peter followed at a distance.

⁵⁵ But when they had kindled a fire in the middle of the courtyard and had sat down together, Peter sat down with them.

⁵⁶ A servant girl saw him seated there in the firelight. She looked closely at him and said, "This man was with him."

⁵⁷ But he denied it. "Woman, I don't know him," he said.

⁵⁸ A little later someone else saw him and said, "You also are one of them."

"Man, I am not!" Peter replied.

⁵⁹ About an hour later another asserted, "Certainly this fellow was with him, for he is a Galilean."

⁶⁰ *Peter replied, "Man, I don't know what you're talking about!" Just as he was speaking, the rooster crowed.*

⁶¹ *The Lord turned and looked straight at Peter. Then Peter remembered the word the Lord had spoken to him: "Before the rooster crows today, you will disown me three times."*

⁶² *And he went outside and wept bitterly.*

MEDITATION

How do you think Peter felt knowing he denied his Savior? Why did it hurt? When have you felt that way? What are some of the ways you've betrayed Jesus in your everyday life?

[Pause to journal.]

Now read about a later encounter between Jesus and

Peter from John 21:15-19:

¹⁵ When they had finished eating, Jesus said to Simon Peter, "Simon son of John, do you truly love me more than these?"

"Yes, Lord," he said, "you know that I love you."

Jesus said, "Feed my lambs."

¹⁶ Again Jesus said, "Simon son of John, do you truly love me?"

He answered, "Yes, Lord, you know that I love you."

Jesus said, "Take care of my sheep."

¹⁷ The third time he said to him, "Simon son of John, do you love me?"

Peter was hurt because Jesus asked him the third time, "Do you love me?" He said, "Lord, you know all things; you know that I love you."

Jesus said, "Feed my sheep.

¹⁸ I tell you the truth, when you were younger you dressed yourself and went where you wanted; but when you are old you will stretch out your hands, and someone else will dress you and lead you where you do not want to go."

¹⁹ Jesus said this to indicate the kind of death by which Peter would glorify God. Then he said to him, "Follow me!"

Replay this episode in your mind as you read the passage again. But this time imagine it's *you* standing on the beach, and it's you to whom Jesus is speaking. What is he saying to you? What is your response? Write out how you think the conversation would go.

FURTHER ON, DEEPER IN

Use the space below to share your own thoughts and reflections.

COMPANIONS ON THE JOURNEY

O HOLY SPIRIT, DESCEND PLENTIFULLY INTO MY HEART. ENLIGHTEN THE DARK CORNERS OF THIS NEGLECTED DWELLING, AND SCATTER THERE THY CHEERFUL BEAMS.

—ST. AUGUSTINE (354-430), PHILOSOPHER AND BISHOP OF HIPPO
CONFESSIONS

DAY 21

LISTENING

Genesis 1:26-31

26 Then God said, *"Let us make man in our image, in our likeness,* and let them rule over the fish of the sea and the birds of the air, over the livestock, over all the earth, and over all the creatures that move along the ground."

27 So *God created man in his own image, in the image of God he created him; male and female he created them.*

28 God blessed them and said to them, "Be fruitful and increase in number; fill the earth and subdue it. Rule over the fish of the sea and the birds of the air and over every living creature that moves on the ground."

29 Then God said, "I give you every seed-bearing plant on the face of the whole earth and every tree that has fruit with seed in it. They will be yours for food.

30 And to all the beasts of the earth and all the birds of the air and all the creatures that move on the ground— everything that has the breath of life in it—I give every green plant for food." And it was so.

31 *God saw all that he had made, and it was very good.* And there was evening, and there was morning—the sixth day.

MEDITATION

Begin your time of reflection by taking three deep breaths. If you can, touch a place on your body where you're able to feel your heartbeat. (You can use two fingers to find your pulse on your wrist, at the base of your neck, or at your temples— or just place your hand over your heart.) Take a moment to feel your pulse. It's a remarkable rhythm. The rhythm of life. The Morse code of your body signaling that you're alive.

But how did you get here? Was it by chance—a mere roll of the biological dice? Was it simply the by-product of two human beings joined together by a sexual act? Was it nothing more than another step in the inevitable march of human history?

No.

God made you in his image. *God made you in his image.* It's an amazing thought. As you consider those words, try the following meditation exercise. Read the following phrase five times. Each time you read it, emphasize a different word. And each time, come to a full stop, and let your mind and heart inhale the full truth of what you've read.

God made me in his image.

God *made* me in his image.

God made *me* in his image.

God made me in *his* image.

God made me in his *image.*

Are you comprehending this truth? You're not an accident. There is a grand design in your being brought to life. Not only did God think your creation was good, he thought it was "very good."

Breathe deeply again. Fill your lungs with the God–given air that's available to his very good creation. Try to breathe in the wonder of being created as a grand design, in the image of the Grand Designer.

In the following space, journal your feelings about which of the five "God made" statements means the most to you. Which statement carries with it the greatest sense of mystery? Which offers the greatest word of challenge?

FURTHER ON, DEEPER IN

Use the space below to share your own thoughts and reflections.

COMPANIONS ON THE JOURNEY

O LORD, THAT LENDS ME LIFE, LEND ME A HEART REPLETE
WITH THANKFULNESS!

—WILLIAM SHAKESPEARE (1564-1616), ENGLISH AUTHOR
HENRY VI, PART II

DAY 22

LISTENING

Psalm 37:3-7

3 Trust in the Lord and do good; dwell in the land and enjoy safe pasture.

4 Delight yourself in the Lord and he will give you the desires of your heart.

5 Commit your way to the Lord; trust in him and he will do this:

6 He will make your righteousness shine like the dawn, the justice of your cause like the noonday sun.

7 *Be still before the Lord* and wait patiently for him; do not fret when men succeed in their ways, when they carry out their wicked schemes.

MEDITATION

Take three deep breaths and then put your body in a comfortable position. You may want to sit or kneel. Whatever your position, place yourself physically and mentally in a posture of *stillness* and *silence*. Repeat this phrase a few times: "Be still before the Lord." Let the words wash over you like a hot, pulsing shower, relaxing and cleansing you. Wait patiently for the Lord.

No movement...no thoughts...just God. Give him space. Give him time. Be still. Wait.

[Wait patiently.]

What do you hear in the silence? Do you sense God's presence? Do you hear the sound of your own breathing? Do you hear street noises outside your window? Do you hear your family members talking? Do you hear the sounds of your house—a clock, a furnace, a dishwasher? Or was your silence interrupted by the voice of your own mind, demanding attention to the day's plans, replaying conversations from yesterday, rehearsing your lines for today's "performance"?

Waiting on anything in a world that constantly urges us to hurry is one of the hardest disciplines of going deep with God. First, it's hard because it requires patience. Second, it's hard because there are so many noises and pseudo-urgencies that seem to drown out God's voice in our lives. And third, it's hard because, if we're honest, we're probably waiting on something or someone else to bring us the "desires" of our hearts.

Try again to go to your quiet place. Be still. Be quiet.

Take three deep breaths as you begin. Each time you breathe in, whisper this simple prayer: "Speak, Lord, to me. You are my delight. You are my desire." And with each breath you exhale, think of yourself drawing away from the distractions that keep you from God—moving beyond the sound barrier of demanding thoughts and misplaced desires. Then, in the following space, write your thoughts about your time with God.

Be willing to wait patiently. God will give you the desires of your heart.

FURTHER ON, DEEPER IN

Use the space below to share your own thoughts and reflections.

COMPANIONS ON THE JOURNEY

THE THOUGHT OF YOU [GOD] STIRS MANKIND SO DEEPLY THAT HE CAN-
NOT BE CONTENT UNLESS HE PRAISES YOU, BECAUSE YOU MADE US FOR
YOURSELF AND OUR HEARTS FIND NO PEACE UNTIL THEY REST IN YOU.

—ST. AUGUSTINE (354-430), PHILOSOPHER AND BISHOP OF HIPPO
CONFESSIONS

DAY 23

LISTENING

John 20:11-18

11 But Mary stood outside the tomb crying. As she wept, she bent over to look into the tomb

12 and saw two angels in white, seated where Jesus' body had been, one at the head and the other at the foot.

13 They asked her, "Woman, why are you crying?"

"They have taken my Lord away," she said, "and I don't know where they have put him."

14 At this, she turned around and saw Jesus standing there, but she did not realize that it was Jesus.

15 "Woman," he said, "why are you crying? Who is it you are looking for?"

Thinking he was the gardener, she said, "Sir, if you have carried him away, tell me where you have put him, and I will get him."

16 Jesus said to her, "Mary."

She turned toward him and cried out in Aramaic, "Rabboni!" (which means Teacher).

17 Jesus said, *"Do not hold on to me, for I have not yet returned to the Father. Go instead to my brothers and tell them, 'I am returning to my Father and your Father, to my God and your God.'"*

18 Mary Magdalene went to the disciples with the news: "I have seen the Lord!" And she told them that he had said these things to her.

MEDITATION

Jesus gave Mary a strange rebuke: "Do not hold on to me, for I have not yet returned to the Father."

Take a moment to imagine yourself standing face to face with Jesus that first Easter morning as he speaks these words to you: "Don't cling to me, because I've not yet returned to the Father."

What are you feeling? Is it alarm? Hurt? Shame? Embarrassment? Fear? Or maybe...wonder?

What was Jesus saying to Mary in the awe and confusion surrounding his empty tomb? Perhaps he was telling her, "Mary, there's so much more to this story than you know, so much more of this picture you don't see. You are standing knee deep in waters that go much deeper. By clinging to what you know, you may miss out on what you have yet to discover."

Mary knew Jesus as "Rabonni" (Teacher). Maybe you know him as a friend or a co-pilot or a person you talk about at youth group. Or maybe you know him as a nice, moral teacher—kind of a Yoda-meets-Mr. Rogers.

But what if your desire to cling to what you know about Jesus is exactly what stands in the way of your getting to know him better? What if Christ's desire is to introduce you to a completely new dimension of who he is? What if his desire is to be more for you than you now know him to be?

And why are we are so prone to cling to safe, comfortable notions of Jesus?

As you sit comfortably and read these words, picture yourself looking into the face of Jesus. Don't hurry through this encounter. Then explore the landscape of the empty tomb. What do you see? What do you hear? Can you hear, perhaps, the Spirit of God saying, "There is so much more to know, so much more to see—don't cling"?

As you journal in the following space, do you have any sense of how Jesus might want to open to you a story bigger than the one you've known, a picture bigger than the one you've seen—a Jesus deeper and more awesome than you now know him to be.

FURTHER ON, DEEPER IN

Use the space below to share your own thoughts and reflections.

COMPANIONS ON THE JOURNEY

ONE DOES NOT DISCOVER NEW LANDS WITHOUT CONSENTING TO LOSE
SIGHT OF THE SHORE FOR A VERY LONG TIME.

—ANDRÉ GIDE (1869-1951), FRENCH AUTHOR
THE COUNTERFEITERS

DAY 24

LISTENING

Psalm 40:1-17

1 I waited patiently for the Lord; he turned to me and heard my cry.

2 *He lifted me out of the slimy pit, out of the mud and mire; he set my feet on a rock and gave me a firm place to stand.*

3 He put a new song in my mouth, a hymn of praise to our God. Many will see and fear and put their trust in the Lord.

4 Blessed is the man who makes the Lord his trust, who does not look to the proud, to those who turn aside to false gods.

5 Many, O Lord my God, are the wonders you have done. The things you planned for us no one can recount to you; were I to speak and tell of them, they would be too many to declare.

6 Sacrifice and offering you did not desire, but my ears you have pierced; burnt offerings and sin offerings you did not require.

7 Then I said, "Here I am, I have come—it is written about me in the scroll.

8 I desire to do your will, O my God; your law is within my heart."

9 I proclaim righteousness in the great assembly; I do not seal my lips, as you know, O Lord.

10 I do not hide your righteousness in my heart; I speak of your faithfulness and salvation. I do not conceal your love and your truth from the great assembly.

11 Do not withhold your mercy from me, O Lord; may your love and your truth always protect me.

12 For troubles without number surround me; my sins have overtaken me, and I cannot see.

They are more than the hairs of my head, and my heart fails within me.

13 Be pleased, O Lord, to save me; O Lord, come quickly to help me.

14 May all who seek to take my life be put to shame and confusion; may all who desire my ruin be turned back in disgrace.

15 May those who say to me, "Aha! Aha!" be appalled at their own shame.

16 But may all who seek you rejoice and be glad in you; may those who love your salvation always say, "The Lord be exalted!"

17 Yet I am poor and needy; may the Lord think of me. You are my help and my deliverer; O my God, do not delay.

MEDITATION

As you begin this exercise of meditation, try to think of five words or phrases that describe your life. Write them in the space at the end of this meditation.

Are there any words or phrases in Psalm 40 you can "borrow" to describe your life? If so, circle them in the previous passage.

In this psalm one of the most vivid images David uses to describe his life is a pit—a deep, dark, empty place with no pleasant way in and no easy way out. Do you ever have similar thoughts—as though you're trapped in a dark, lonely place?

What is it in your life that makes your pit so deep and discouraging? Is it a particular event? A relationship? An inability or inadequacy you feel keenly? Picture it in your mind. Allow your imagination to pan the dim horizons of your pit. Hold on to that picture. Force yourself to feel fully the depths of that place.

Now, without moving from that place, add Jesus to the picture. Imagine him there with you stepping out of the darkness with arms open wide. Not calling you from outside the pit, but actually in the pit with you.

As you envision the Christ who is willing to go with you even into your darkest places, consider these words from Ephesians 4:7-10:

> 7 But to each one of us grace has been given as Christ apportioned it.
> 8 This is why it says:
> "When he ascended on high,
> he led captives in his train
> and gave gifts to men."
> 9 (What does "he ascended" mean except that he also descended to the lower, earthly regions?
> 10 He who descended is the very one who ascended higher than all the heavens, in order to fill the whole universe.)

Can you hear Jesus say to you today, "And surely I am with you always, to the very end of the age." (Matthew 28:20)? Can you hear him tell you he wants to lift you out of your pit? Think about that. He's not commanding you to climb out on your own so he can embrace you. He's asking you to let him *lift you out!*

As you pray over these questions, use the following space to write your own psalm to God. Don't try to make it sound like other psalms. Try to make it sound like you. As you write your words, try to visualize a dark place made brighter by the very real presence of the One who is the Light of Life.

FURTHER ON, DEEPER IN

Use the space below to share your own thoughts and reflections.

COMPANIONS ON THE JOURNEY

THERE IS NO PIT SO DEEP THAT GOD IS NOT DEEPER STILL.

—CORRIE TEN BOOM (1892-1983)
DUTCH EVANGELIST AND CONCENTRATION-CAMP SURVIVOR
THE HIDING PLACE

DAY 25

LISTENING

Jeremiah 20:7-13

7 O Lord, you deceived me, and I was deceived; you overpowered me and prevailed. I am ridiculed all day long; everyone mocks me.

8 Whenever I speak, I cry out proclaiming violence and destruction. So the word of the Lord has brought me insult and reproach all day long.

9 But if I say, "I will not mention him or speak any more in his name," his word is in my heart like a fire, a fire shut up in my bones. I am weary of holding it in; indeed, I cannot.

10 I hear many whispering, "Terror on every side! Report him! Let's report him!" All my friends are waiting for me to slip, saying, "Perhaps he will be deceived; then we will prevail over him and take our revenge on him."

11 *But the Lord is with me like a mighty warrior; so my persecutors will stumble and not prevail. They will fail and be thoroughly disgraced; their dishonor will never be forgotten.*

12 O Lord Almighty, you who examine the righteous and probe the heart and mind, let me see your vengeance upon them, for to you I have committed my cause.

13 Sing to the Lord! Give praise to the Lord! He rescues the life of the needy from the hands of the wicked.

MEDITATION

Begin by reading this passage slowly three times. Then sit quietly for a few minutes. Before you read anything else, quietly ponder these words: "O Lord, you deceived me, and I was deceived; you overpowered me and prevailed."

[Pause to read.]

The New Jerusalem Bible translates verse 7 this way: "O Lord, Thou hast seduced me and I was seduced; Thou hast overcome me and prevailed." It's one of those verses you have to read twice. After all, it's not every day you read "Thou" and "seduced" in the same sentence! But, in fact, "seduced" is probably closer to what Jeremiah was feeling.

It's like Jeremiah is saying, "I was deceived. I was seduced. I didn't bargain for all this when I responded to the call of God." But then, the more he experienced the intensity of God's passionate love, the more he was drawn to it, the more he was captivated by it, the more it began to beat with intensity in his own heart.

But that passionate love comes with a cost. It did for Jeremiah and it likely will for us. Consider some of the following comments:

- "I've become a laughingstock."

- "Everyone mocks me."

- "People think I'm some kind of weird religious freak."

- "My friends want to know why I'm not sleeping with my boyfriend/girlfriend."

- "People think I'm stupid, because I wasn't willing to cheat on the test."

- "People don't get it when I invite them to church with me."

Have you, as a Christian, ever felt that sense of "Oh my gosh, what have I gotten myself into?"

Stop for a moment as you ponder that question. Allow God to meet you in the midst of your feelings, even if they are feelings of deception and betrayal.

Imagine God holding those feelings in his hands. Imagine yourself holding in your heart the intensity of his love (like a "fire shut up in my bones," as Jeremiah put it). You may want to stop to write down some of what you're feeling.

[Pause to journal.]

In spite of his frustration with God, Jeremiah writes "the Lord is with me like a mighty warrior." The great news in all of this is that God is with you in the midst of the craziness. He will not lead you where he will not go. You will not speak by yourself. You will not go alone. This is not a God who "loves 'em and leaves 'em." You may have been seduced, but you have not been deceived.

God is there with you all the time.

God is there with you.

God is there.

God is.

Take a few moments to savor this truth by closing your eyes and meditating on the phrase, "The Lord is with me like a mighty warrior."

FURTHER ON, DEEPER IN

Use the space below to share your own thoughts and reflections.

COMPANIONS ON THE JOURNEY

IF YOU BELIEVE WHAT YOU LIKE IN THE GOSPEL AND REJECT WHAT YOU DON'T LIKE, IT IS NOT THE GOSPEL YOU BELIEVE, BUT YOURSELF.

—ST. AUGUSTINE (354-430), PHILOSOPHER AND BISHOP OF HIPPO

DAY 26

LISTENING

Luke 19:1-10

1 Jesus entered Jericho and was passing through.

2 A man was there by the name of Zacchaeus; he was a chief tax collector and was wealthy.

3 He wanted to see who Jesus was, but being a short man he could not, because of the crowd.

4 So he ran ahead and climbed a sycamore-fig tree to see him, since Jesus was coming that way.

5 *When Jesus reached the spot, he looked up and said to him, "Zacchaeus, come down immediately. I must stay at your house today."*

6 *So he came down at once and welcomed him gladly.*

7 All the people saw this and began to mutter, "He has gone to be the guest of a 'sinner.'"

8 But Zacchaeus stood up and said to the Lord, "Look, Lord! Here and now I give half of my possessions to the poor, and if I have cheated anybody out of anything, I will pay back four times the amount."

9 Jesus said to him, "Today salvation has come to this house, because this man, too, is a son of Abraham.

10 For the Son of Man came to seek and to save what was lost."

MEDITATION

Read this remarkable episode played out on the dusty streets of downtown Jericho. Imagine you're the one in the tree. From a long way off you can see Jesus coming toward your perch.

You've wanted to see Jesus for a long time. But what are you feeling as he approaches? Are you hiding? If so, from whom? And why? In what ways do you feel as though your life is "out on a limb"? What are some of the feelings that make you want to stay up in that tree?

No doubt, part of what made Zacchaeus reluctant to climb down were the faces of the townspeople who looked up at him. Are there any people whose faces keep you up in your tree? If so, who are they? Why do they make you uneasy about climbing down?

What thoughts, fears, or prejudices do you think Zacchaeus had to lay aside in order to have this encounter with Jesus? What might those thoughts, fears, and prejudices be in your life?

Consider the difference between the "before" Zacchaeus who was waiting in the tree to see Jesus, and the "after" Zacchaeus who actually encountered Jesus. What difference do you think meeting Jesus made in Zacchaeus' life? What difference has meeting Jesus made in your life? What areas of your life is Jesus asking you to make right? How can you begin to do that?

Jot down your reflections.

FURTHER ON, DEEPER IN

Use the space below and on the following page to share your own thoughts and reflections.

COMPANIONS ON THE JOURNEY

PRAYER IS THE LAYING ASIDE OF THOUGHTS.

—EVAGRIUS PONTICUS (345-399), EARLY CHRISTIAN MONK AND
THEOLOGIAN "ON PRAYER 61," IN THE PHILOKALIA

DAY 27

LISTENING

Psalm 34:1-18

1 I will extol the Lord at all times; his praise will always be on my lips.

2 My soul will boast in the Lord; let the afflicted hear and rejoice.

3 Glorify the Lord with me; let us exalt his name together.

4 I sought the Lord, and he answered me; he delivered me from all my fears.

5 Those who look to him are radiant; their faces are never covered with shame.

6 This poor man called, and the Lord heard him; he saved him out of all his troubles.

7 The angel of the Lord encamps around those who fear him, and he delivers them.

8 *Taste* and see that the Lord is good; blessed is the man who takes refuge in him.

9 *Fear* the Lord, you his saints, for those who fear him lack nothing.

10 The lions may grow weak and hungry, but those who seek the Lord lack no good thing.

11 *Come*, my children, listen to me; I will teach you the fear of the Lord.

12 Whoever of you loves life and desires to see many good days,

13 *keep* your tongue from evil and your lips from speaking lies.

14 *Turn* from evil and do good; seek peace and pursue it.

15 The eyes of the Lord are on the righteous and his ears are attentive to their cry;

16 the face of the Lord is against those who do evil,
    to cut off the memory of them from the earth.

17 The righteous cry out, and the Lord hears them; he delivers them from all their troubles.

[18] *The Lord is close to the brokenhearted and saves those who are crushed in spirit.*

MEDITATION

You'll need a spare piece of paper to begin this exercise. Crumple the paper, crush it, maybe even step on it. Then take a good look at what remains.

Have you ever had a day, a week, or a season when that seemed to be the state of your spirit: broken, misshapen, crushed, and creased? Are you feeling that way now? Who or what crushes you? Is it the stress of school? The pressures of a job? The tensions of family relationships? The ups and downs of friendship? The guilt of sin?

Look at the crushed piece of paper and think about your own spirit. Maybe you feel frustration...or disgust... or sadness...or rebellion...or emptiness. Whatever it is you feel, allow yourself to feel it fully. Don't run or hide from your feelings. Perhaps you feel joyful today. Or maybe your heart is heavy. Perhaps you've been too busy to allow yourself to feel anything lately. Or, maybe, you've felt, as a Christian, you don't have any right to feel certain things. But, for right now, know that in God's presence you have the freedom to feel anything—whether you feel peaceful and whole, or creased, crushed, torn, and twisted. In the following space, write down what you're feeling today.

[Pause to journal.]

David wrote Psalm 34 in a time of dark despair when he was facing grave danger and constant trouble. In fact, he wrote the words after he'd faked insanity so his enemy Abimilech (also called Achish) would not kill him. (For more info on the story, check out 1 Samuel 21:10-15.) Yet, though David was fearful and fragile, he was able to cling to one certainty: "The Lord is close to the brokenhearted."

Read the passage slowly two or three times. Meditate especially on David's final words, "The Lord is close to the brokenhearted and saves those who are crushed in spirit" (verse 18).

Find your trashed piece of paper and spread it out again. Write on it the five key words in this passage—words that offer help and encouragement to us when we are brokenhearted:

- "Taste" (verse 8)
- "Fear" (verse 9)
- "Come" (verse 11)
- "keep" (verse 13)
- "Turn" (verse 14).

Put the piece of paper some place where you'll see it on a regular basis. Let it remind you "The Lord is close to the brokenhearted and saves those who are crushed in spirit."

FURTHER ON, DEEPER IN:

Use the space below and on the following page to share your own thoughts and reflections.

112 :: **ENJOY** THE SILENCE

COMPANIONS ON THE JOURNEY

MAKE READY FOR THE CHRIST, WHOSE SMILE, LIKE LIGHTNING,
SETS FREE THE SONG OF EVERLASTING GLORY, THAT NOW SLEEPS,
IN YOUR PAPER FLESH, LIKE DYNAMITE.

—THOMAS MERTON (1915-1968), TRAPPIST MONK
"THE VICTORY," *COLLECTED POEMS*

DAY 28

LISTENING

John 13:5-11

5 *After that, he poured water into a basin and began to wash his disciples' feet, drying them with the towel that was wrapped around him.*

6 *He came to Simon Peter, who said to him, "Lord, are you going to wash my feet?"*

7 Jesus replied, "You do not realize now what I am doing, but later you will understand."

8 "No," said Peter, "you shall never wash my feet." Jesus answered, "Unless I wash you, you have no part with me."

9 "Then, Lord," Simon Peter replied, "not just my feet but my hands and my head as well!"

10 Jesus answered, "A person who has had a bath needs only to wash his feet; his whole body is clean. And you are clean, though not every one of you."

11 For he knew who was going to betray him, and that was why he said not every one was clean.

MEDITATION

Read this passage slowly and thoughtfully. You'll see Jesus is washing the disciples' feet. We know Jesus spoke to Peter. We even know the gist of what he said. We don't know if he spoke to the other disciples or what he might have said to them.

Imagine you're in that upper room. Jesus is coming to wash your feet. What does he say to you? How do you respond? Can you feel his rough, carpenter's hands holding your feet? What do his hands feel like? How do you feel about those hands washing your feet?

Can you feel the water on your tired, dusty feet? Think about the places you've walked and what you might be carrying from your journey. Peter seemed to blurt out his words of protest, "You shall never wash my feet." What words come to your mind as you look into the face of this God-become-servant?

Write your thoughts about what might take place.

FURTHER ON, DEEPER IN

Use the space below to share your own thoughts and reflections.

COMPANIONS ON THE JOURNEY

WHEN WE WERE GIVEN THE CAPACITY TO LOVE, TO SPEAK, TO DECIDE, TO DREAM, TO HOPE AND CREATE AND SUFFER, WE WERE ALSO GIVEN THE LONGING TO BE KNOWN BY THE ONE WHO MOST WANTS TO BE COMPLETELY KNOWN. IT IS A LONGING WOVEN INTO THE VERY FABRIC OF THE IMAGE IN WHICH WE WERE MADE.

—ROBERT BENSON (BORN 1952), U.S. AUTHOR
BETWEEN THE DREAMING AND THE COMING TRUE

DAY 29

LISTENING

Matthew 15:22-28

22 A Canaanite woman from that vicinity came to him, crying out, "Lord, Son of David, have mercy on me! My daughter is suffering terribly from demon-possession."

23 *Jesus did not answer a word.* So his disciples came to him and urged him, "Send her away, for she keeps crying out after us."

24 He answered, "I was sent only to the lost sheep of Israel."

25 The woman came and knelt before him. "Lord, help me!" she said.

26 He replied, "It is not right to take the children's bread and toss it to their dogs."

27 "Yes, Lord," she said, "but even the dogs eat the crumbs that fall from their masters' table."

28 Then Jesus answered, "Woman, you have great faith! Your request is granted." And her daughter was healed from that very hour.

MEDITATION

There's a remarkable sentence in this passage: "Jesus did not answer a word" (verse 23). There's no silence so deep as the silence of God.

Have you ever been there? Have you ever experienced that depth of silence? Has there ever been a time in your life when you've brought a need or desire before God and you heard...*nothing*. No words of comfort. No reassuring answer. No miraculous intervention. Just silence.

Think about such a time. As you recall it, how are you feeling? Angry? Sad? Insignificant? Forgotten? Do you feel sorry for yourself? What is your sense of God in that place of silence?

[Pause to journal.]

How does God's silence affect your prayerful requests to him? Do you just turn your back and choose not to ask again? Do you hear the voices of the disciples saying, "Send her away" (verse 23)? Do you feel rejected, unheard, unwanted, unloved, betrayed? Do you feel as though maybe it's better to walk away from the whole thing? After all, surrender doesn't hurt as much as outright rejection.

Before you answer, look at what the woman in the story did.

She didn't walk away. She didn't surrender to despair and cynicism. Instead she kept crying out after Jesus and his disciples.

Go back and read verse 24. You'll see that, after the silence, Jesus answered the woman. And in some ways, Jesus' first words to the woman may have felt even worse than his silence. He didn't heal her daughter immediately as she'd hoped he would. It must have felt to her as though his answer ignored her questions, not to mention the pain she felt.

But the woman was persistent, not because of who *she* was, but because of who *he* was—the Christ, the Great Healer. She dropped to her knees in faith and said, "Lord, help me!"

Then Jesus spoke again. And this time, after the silence, it was with a volume echoing all the way back to the sickbed of a little girl in a distant Canaanite village:

"Woman, you have great faith! Your request is granted" (verse 28). And in that moment, her daughter was healed.

We may not always understand those times when it feels as though God is silent. But consider this possibility: In those moments when there is no word, perhaps God is reminding us that, even more than he wants to meet our needs, he wants us to understand our own need to meet him, to fall before him, and to trust him.

Don't hide from the silence of God.

Sit with it.

Ponder it.

Challenge it.

Question it.

But whatever you do, don't mistake it for lack of compassion or lack of hearing.

FURTHER ON, DEEPER IN

Use the space below and on the following page to share your own thoughts and reflections.

COMPANIONS ON THE JOURNEY

LISTEN TO GOD'S SPEECH IN HIS WONDROUS, TERRIBLE, GENTLE, LOVING, ALL-EMBRACING SILENCE.

—CATHERINE DE HUECK DOHERTY (1896-1985),
CATHOLIC LAY APOSTLE AND FOUNDER OF MADONNA HOUSE
CITED IN *THE SUN AND MOON OVER ASSISI* BY GERARD THOMAS STRAUB

DAY 30

LISTENING

Psalm 100:1-5

1 Shout for joy to the Lord, all the earth.
2 Worship the Lord with gladness;
   come before him with joyful songs.
3 Know that the Lord is God.
   It is he who made us, and we are his;
   we are his people, the sheep of his pasture.
4 *Enter his gates with thanksgiving*
   and his courts with praise;
   give thanks to him and praise his name.
5 For the Lord is good and his love endures forever;
   his faithfulness continues through all generations.

MEDITATION

Imagine yourself in a great cathedral. Consider its beauty and grandeur with its high ceilings and magnificent arched windows of stained glass. This is a holy place, a quiet place, a place of depth and mystery.

Now imagine you're still seated in the same sanctuary—only not in the pews, but in the choir loft at the very front of the church. And sitting there in the pews in front of you is God himself. In this worship service, you have an audience of One. Your order of worship is Psalm 100. Take time to pause, pray, write, reflect, and listen as you meet with God in this special place.

"Shout for joy to the Lord, all the earth."

Begin with this thought as you worship God today in your "choir loft," or wherever you are right now. You are joining a chorus of brothers and sisters in Christ all over the globe. A choir of all ages and ethnic groups. A chorus including not only human voices, but the earthly voices of all creation—from the howl of a jackal to the blossom of a sunflower to the splashing of a stream. How amazing is it to realize you're part of such a vast Creation Chorus!

> *"Worship the Lord with gladness;*
> *come before him with joyful songs."*

Why don't you, right now, sing to the Lord your favorite worship song? If you aren't comfortable singing, just pray to him the words of your favorite hymn or song.

> *"Know that the Lord is God."*

Take time now to meditate on one aspect of God's character you've come to appreciate in the past year. It may be his faithfulness...or his power...or his grace...or his mercy...or his wisdom. Worship God now for what you know of him.

> *"It is he who made us, and we are his;*
> *we are his people, the sheep of his pasture."*

We worship God because we belong to God. We are his. Ponder those words a few minutes as you consider what it means for you to be *his*. What does it mean for your life at home, at school, with friends, at church, on the street? What does it mean for you to be "the sheep of his pasture"?

> *"Enter his gates with thanksgiving and his courts with*
> *praise; give thanks to him and praise his name."*

There was only one reason for sheep to be brought into the temple courts: to be offered as sacrifices to God. As you look out from your choir loft today and into the face of God, does it feel like he is worthy of your sacrifice?

What might your sacrifice look like? Is it an attitude, a habit, a relationship, a possession? Imagine yourself stepping down from your loft and taking that offering to the feet of God.

"For the Lord is good and his love endures forever;
his faithfulness continues through all generations."

Close your time of worship with prayer. Focus particularly on the words, "His faithfulness continues."

This may be the end of your quiet time, but it's not the end of your time with God. Watch for him in the hours ahead. Look for him in the mundane moments. Search for him in the faces you pass. Listen for him in the sounds you hear.

There is no place you will be today, tomorrow, or forever that is not his sanctuary.

"Shout for joy to the Lord, all the earth!"

FURTHER ON, DEEPER IN

Use the space below and on the following page to share your own thoughts and reflections.

COMPANIONS ON THE JOURNEY

WE CAN FIRST CONSOLE OURSELVES WITH THE THOUGHT THAT NO
ATTEMPT TO SPEAK WITH GOD, NO MATTER HOW BARREN OUR
SOUL IS, OR HOW FRUSTRATED OUR EFFORTS ARE, IS IN VAIN.
THE UNSUCCESSFUL EFFORT ITSELF IS A PRAYER.

—KILIAN MCDONNELL, OSB (BORN 1921), CATHOLIC PRIEST AND AUTHOR
NOTHING BUT CHRIST: A BENEDICTINE APPROACH TO LAY SPIRITUALITY

AFTERWORD

THE DAY AFTER THIRTY

Every great story involves a quest. In J.R.R. Tolkien's *The Hobbit*, Bilbo Baggins ran from the door at a quarter till eleven without even so much as a pocket handkerchief and launched on an adventure that would change his life forever. Alice stepped through the looking glass into Wonderland. Lucy, Edmund, Susan and Peter stumbled through the wardrobe into Narnia. Abraham left his country, his people, and his father's household to follow the most outlandish sort of promise from a God he'd only just met, and he never came back. Jacob and his sons went to Egypt for some groceries and four hundred years later the Israel nation pulled up stakes and headed for home. Peter, Andrew, James, and John all turned on a dime one day to follow the Master, their fishing nets heaped in wet piles behind them. The Sacred Romance involves for every soul a journey of heroic proportions. And while it may require for some a change of geography, for every soul it means a journey of the heart.

—Brent Curtis and John Eldredge
The Sacred Romance: Drawing Closer to the Heart of God
(Thomas Nelson Publishers)

Thirty readings ago you began a journey of the heart— a journey we hope has brought you nearer to the heart of God. You've traveled this road by way of an ancient vehicle, *lectio divina*, a centuries-old contemplative exercise that has carried many a traveler through the highlands and lowlands of a deeper intimacy with God.

You may have found places along the way where the view was stunning. Other parts of the journey probably felt slow and tedious. Perhaps your trip took you into uncharted territory. Perhaps it offered opportunities to explore new insights. Or maybe your journey took you back to places you thought—maybe even hoped—you'd long since left behind. But whatever twists and turns you've taken on this thirty-day experiment in listening to God, one thing is critical: *Don't let the journey stop here.*

There's one thing you should always remember about the walk of faith: God is much more interested in your direction than in your current position. (If you don't believe us, check out Philippians 3:1-14.) Where you are today in your relationship with God is important. But far more important is where you're headed in your relationship with him.

Here are a few thoughts to keep you moving forward.

1. You can do your own *lectio divina* exercises.

Now that you've learned the basic idea, it's time for the training wheels to come off. You don't need a special book. All you need is a Bible, some time, a quiet place, and an open heart.

Although we've suggested specific words or phrases for you to focus on in these exercises, in true *lectio divina* you would not be given a particular verse to concentrate on. Instead, you would read a selected passage slowly, as you have learned to do in these pages. As you read, listen for a word or phrase God brings to your mind. That word or phrase becomes your focus. It may be a word leading you to thanksgiving... or worship... or confession... or an expression of need. Be sensitive to the Holy Spirit's promptings—wholly listen and then respond.

2. You can choose your own Scripture passages.

In this book we've chosen the Bible readings for you. But as you begin to read and practice on your own, you'll need to choose your own Scripture passages. We suggest you start by working your way through a basic, easy-to-read book like the Gospel of Luke.

There are also many Internet sites that suggest daily Scripture readings suitable for the *lectio divina* process. Among the sites we've found are...

www.dailybible.com

www.rc.net/wcc/readings

www.cresourcei.org/daily.html

You'll find many other possibilities by entering "daily Bible readings" into any Internet search engine.

Remember, meditation involves chewing slowly. The *lectio divina* method is not about gobbling down long passages every day—or working through the entire Bible in three weeks. Pace yourself. For example, you may choose to read 10-20 verses a day as you work through the book. Obviously there will be natural breaks in the text—the end of the parable, the end of a narrative, the end of a chapter—that may affect your verse count. Don't get too hung up on passages you don't understand. Focus on passages you do understand.

If you find yourself totally inspired or perplexed or intrigued by a passage, and you would like to do further study, there are a number of Web sites that can help you with basic insights into the text, including...

www.biblegateway.com

www.gospelcom.net

www.studylight.org

3. You can do this!

Spiritual disciplines like *lectio divina* are not easy to practice, even when you're developing a habit. They're called *disciplines* for the same reason physical exercises are called *workouts*. They require work. But they are worth the effort.

We've talked about *lectio divina* as the practice of carving out time in a loud world to be quiet and listen to our loving God. The word *carving* is significant. It suggests effort, care, intention, and process. A chunk of marble doesn't become an angelic figure overnight. Be patient with yourself as you practice these disciplines. Some days you may feel your carving has produced little more than dust and shavings. Other days you'll begin to see in the carving the face of the Rock himself. Don't give up if every day isn't an epiphany—a thunder and lightning thrill show of God's presence.

You might find it helpful to meet on a regular basis with two or three other friends who are willing to embark on this journey with you. Meeting together to share and pray may be a way to build some accountability into your commitment (see Hebrews 10:24-25).

4. You can count on this.

One thing is certain: God wants to speak to us more than we want to listen. Remember, this is a God who has gone to unimaginable lengths to reveal himself to us. If we are willing to listen, and *if we learn how to hear,* God will not be silent.

God's great desire for each of us is not that we practice spiritual disciplines. His primary concern is not that we pray, bow down, raise our arms, genuflect, high five, or hang ten. He's not preoccupied with whether we practice quiet time, Bible study, prayer walks, *lectio, gelato,* or *latte.* His passion is that we draw near to him. And that's huge!

This is not a journey to Jesus; it's a journey *with* Jesus. He's not at the end of the road saying, "Do all this, go to these lengths, and then I will love you." He's not at the beginning of the journey saying, "Have a great trip. Good luck. Don't forget to write." Jesus *is* the journey.

Jesus said, "I am the way and the truth and the life" (John 14:6). He is with us at the beginning of the journey. He is with us at the end of the journey. And he is with us at every point along the way.

We need to learn to grip his hand, better and more tightly, as we continue on this journey together.

SCRIPTURE INDEX